S0-ACB-377

The Making
of a Premier

Westview Replica Editions

The concept of Westview Replica Editions is a response to the continuing crisis in academic and informational publishing. Library budgets for books have been severely curtailed. Ever larger portions of general library budgets are being diverted from the purchase of books and used for data banks, computers, micromedia, and other methods of information retrieval. Interlibrary loan structures further reduce the edition sizes required to satisfy the needs of the scholarly community. Economic pressures on the university presses and the few private scholarly publishing companies have severely limited the capacity of the industry to properly serve the academic and research communities. As a result, many manuscripts dealing with important subjects, often representing the highest level of scholarship, are no longer economically viable publishing projects--or, if accepted for publication, are typically subject to lead times ranging from one to three years.

Westview Replica Editions are our practical solution to the problem. We accept a manuscript in camera-ready form, typed according to our specifications, and move it immediately into the production process. As always, the selection criteria include the importance of the subject, the work's contribution to scholarship, and its insight, originality of thought, and excellence of exposition. The responsibility for editing and proofreading lies with the author or sponsoring institution. We prepare chapter headings and display pages, file for copyright, and obtain Library of Congress Cataloging in Publication Data. A detailed manual contains simple instructions for preparing the final typescript, and our editorial staff is always available to answer questions.

The end result is a book printed on acid-free paper and bound in sturdy library-quality soft covers. We manufacture these books ourselves using equipment that does not require a lengthy make-ready process and that allows us to publish first editions of 300 to 600 copies and to reprint even smaller quantities as needed. Thus, we can produce Replica Editions quickly and can keep even very specialized books in print as long as there is a demand for them.

About the Book and Author

The Making of a Premier:
Zhao Ziyang's Provincial Career
David L. Shambaugh

How did Zhao Ziyang rise through the provincial apparatus of the Chinese Communist Party to become premier in 1980? How did he develop the policies of economic reform in the provinces that have now become national policy? What does Zhao Ziyang's professional development indicate about upward elite mobility in the Chinese political system? These are the central questions the author addresses in this political biography, tracing Zhao Ziyang's career in detail from his youth, through the Anti-Japanese War, the 1949 revolution, land reform, a series of political and economic campaigns during the 1950s and 1960s, the Cultural Revolution, political rehabilitation, and the "Sichuan Experience." Mr. Shambaugh goes beyond a chronological account to elucidate Zhao's job responsibilities and performance, political and economic philosophy, survival strategies, and behavior during thirty tumultous years in provincial politics. Bringing forth much new information drawn extensively from primary source materials, he also provides insights into the functioning of the post-1949 Chinese political system, especially the interplay between central and provincial politics.

David L. Shambaugh, a doctoral candidate in political science at The University of Michigan, has analyzed Chinese and Asian affairs for the U.S. Senate, Department of State, and National Security Council. His articles on Chinese domestic politics, foreign policy, and military affairs have appeared in several scholarly journals and books.

Zhao Ziyang in Sichuan Province, February 1980.

The Making of a Premier

Zhao Ziyang's Provincial Career

David L. Shambaugh

Westview Press / Boulder, Colorado

HOUSTON PUBLIC LIBRARY

R0152005925
SSC

A Westview Replica Edition

All rights reserved. No part of this publication may be reproduced or
transmitted in any form or by any means, electronic or mechanical, including
photocopy, recording, or any information storage and retrieval system,
without permission in writing from the publisher.

Copyright © 1984 by Westview Press, Inc.

Published in 1984 in the United States of America by
    Westview Press, Inc.
    5500 Central Avenue
    Boulder, Colorado 80301
    Frederick A. Praeger, Publisher

Library of Congress Catalog Card Number: 84-50031
ISBN 0-86531-831-X

Printed and bound in the United States of America
10 9 8 7 6 5 4 3 2

For My Parents,
George and Genevieve Shambaugh

Contents

Abbreviations

AFP	Agence France Presse
APC	Agricultural Producers' Cooperative
BAC	Basic Accounting Unit
CASS	Chinese Academy of Social Sciences
CB	Current Background
CCP	Chinese Communist Party
CCP-CC	Chinese Communist Party Central Committee
CPPCC	Chinese People's Political Consultative Conference
CRSG	Cultural Revolution Small Group
CSPS	Chengdu, Sichuan Provincial Service
CYL	Communist Youth League
FBIS	Foreign Broadcast Information Service
GMRB	Guangming Ribao
GPD	PLA General Political Department
JPRS	Joint Publications Research Service
LAPC	Lower Agricultural Producers' Cooperative
MAT	Mutual Aid Team
MD	Military District
MR	Military Region
NCNA	New China News Agency
NFRB	Nanfang Ribao
NPC	National People's Congress
PLA	People's Liberation Army
PLMPA	Poor and Lower Middle Peasants' Association
PRC	People's Republic of China
RGP	Red Guard Press
RMRB	Renmin Ribao
SCMM	Survey Mainland China Magazines
SCMP	Survey Mainland China Press
SCRB	Sichuan Ribao
SEM	Socialist Education Movement
URS	Union Research Service
WTO	Warsaw Treaty Organization
XHDS	Xinhua Domestic Service
YCWB	Yangcheng Wanbao

Preface

This study has evolved through two stages. During the summer of 1980, while I was studying in China, rumors were rampant that Mao's successor Hua Guofeng was on his way out of power, and that Zhao Ziyang would replace him as Premier of the State Council. Zhao was generally thought to have the inside track on the job because he had Deng Xiaoping's support and had administered a series of successful economic reforms in Sichuan province during his tenure there as first Party secretary. These reforms had collectively become known as the "Sichuan Experience," and were being touted for national emulation. Despite the publicity these reforms had received, Zhao remained a rather enigmatic figure to Chinese and foreigners alike. Thus my initial reason for undertaking this study was to provide a clearer picture of the man who was to become one of China's national leaders and of his reformist policies, later to become national policies.

After returning to the United States and concluding the study of Zhao's "Sichuan Experience," it soon became apparent that understanding Zhao's four years in Sichuan would provide only a partial understanding of who he was, what he stood for, and what might be expected from him as a national leader. After all, Zhao's political career did not begin in Sichuan nor were the policies he implemented there without precedent. Thus the second stage of the study entailed researching Zhao's pre-Sichuan life and political career. This comprehensive approach afforded the opportunity to posit some broader hypotheses about what it takes to get to the top of the Chinese political system. These propositions are set forth in the last chapter of this volume. Of course, a single case study is hardly optimal by social science standards, but it is my contention that Zhao Ziyang's career is illustrative of upwardly mobile Chinese elites.

This study has evolved over three years. It has repeatedly been prolonged by the discovery of new evidence and the dislocations of graduate school. Throughout this period, and on multiple drafts of the manuscript, Michel Oksenberg has offered his constructive criticism. Several sections reflect his input. David M. Lampton and Kenneth Lieberthal also provided valuable comments on an earlier draft. I also wish to thank Barbara Congelosi for her editing, Iain Johnston for helping with the index, Yeung Sai-cheung for his research assistance, Lorraine Sobson for her typing, and Diane Scherer for seeing the manuscript through its final stages. Lastly, but by no means least important, has been the unswerving support for this project from my wife Ingrid. She has had to endure all of the frustrations, and now deserves to share the joy of a first book.

David L. Shambaugh
Ann Arbor, Michigan

Introduction

This study is a political biography. My primary purpose has been to trace Zhao Ziyang's career development from birth to his appointment as Premier in 1980. Therefore, the bulk of this volume is a chronological account of Zhao's career in the provinces. Secondly, I have tried to place Zhao's career in the broader context of elite mobility in the Chinese political system.

I argue that, as a provincial elite, Zhao's relationship with the central political authorities (zhongyang) is the crucial variable affecting his career development. Zhao's relationship to the center is manifested in two mediums. The first is Zhao's relationships with his superiors at the provincial, regional, and national levels. Several studies have emphasized the importance of interpersonal relationships (guanxi) and patron-client networks in the Chinese political system.[1] This is by no means unique to China, but perhaps nowhere else is it more pronounced. Zhao's career confirms this point. The second medium is Zhao's response to policies initiated by the center. It has been argued that policy issues are rallying points and loyalty-testing devices for factional alignments, and are only tools for symbolic manipulation by elites.[2] While the former conclusion is no doubt correct, I argue that the latter view seriously underestimates the importance of policy issues as autonomous variables in the policy process, commanding attention in their own right. Policy issues are not abstract symbols, they are at the center of the political process. Politicians worldwide divide and coalesce over policy issues, and expend a great deal of energy and resources in promoting their favorite ones. China is no different in this regard.

For this reason, much of this study is focused on Zhao Ziyang's publicly stated positions on various policy issues. By examining what Zhao says about a particular policy issue we can best exploit the public record and show how his views have changed over time. How Zhao frames an issue can illuminate his personal political philosophy. How Zhao mobilizes support for or against a policy helps to indicate the strength of his political power. How Zhao ultimately implements a policy reveals much about his political work style. Therefore, to the degree possible, given source limitations, I will contrast Zhao's public statements with central policies and will try to determine Zhao's role in the policy implementation process in order to highlight his role in the central-provincial policy process. Throughout this study the reader must bear in mind that the evolution of Zhao's career cannot fully be understood in isolation from the larger central-provincial context. Zhao's job as a provincial official places him at the hub of the policy process. To understand his behavior, therefore, one must be cognizant of the pressures exerted on Zhao from above as well as from below.

The reader must also be aware of the source limitations involved in researching this study. For the period covered in this study China was largely closed to foreigners, especially social science researchers. Without the opportunity to interview Zhao Ziyang or his close associates, one is left with the usual array of sources used in "Pekingological" analysis, e.g.,

— biographical dictionaries;
— public apperance data (compiled in the U.S. Consulate–General Hong Kong biographic card file and National Foreign Assessment Center Appearances of Chinese Leaders);
— central and provincial print media;
— monitored radio broadcasts;
— refugee interviews;
— official statistics;
— Red Guard tabloids; and
— secondary sources.

I have used all of these sources in my research and feel confident that this volume reflects all that we outside of China can presently know about Zhao Ziyang's career. Nonetheless, I believe this to be an incomplete account. As the reader will note, there exist repeated gaps in Zhao's public appearances, and we simply do not know where he was or what he was doing during these periods. Thus the reader must understand that Zhao's repeated "disappearances" are gaps in reporting of his public appearances. Disappearances do not necessarily indicate that Zhao was in political trouble, but simply reflect that he was not reported as appearing publicly during these periods.

With these methodological and source problems in mind, let us proceed to see how Zhao Ziyang rose through the provincial Party apparatus to become China's Premier.

NOTES

1. See for example Lucian Pye, <u>The Dynamics of Chinese Politics</u> (Cambridge, 1981), ch. 7.

2. Ibid.

1
Pre-1953 Training During Wartime and Establishing Credentials in Guangdong: Land Reform and Personnel and Information Management

Zhao Ziyang was born in 1919 in Hua xian (county), Henan province. His father was a landlord who also owned grain storage facilities.[1] Between 1928 and 1937 Zhao successively attended Hua County Number One General Primary School, Kaifeng Number One Junior Middle School, and Wuhan Senior Middle School. In March 1932 Zhao joined the Communist Youth League (CYL), becoming a full member of the Chinese Communist Party (CCP) in February 1938. He joined the CCP in his native Hua county but it is not known who recruited him. He may have subsequently attended a Party school, but he had no form of higher education nor did he travel abroad.

From 1938 to 1940 Zhao served as a CCP secretary in his native Hua xian. During the Japanese invasion this xian became part of the Third Special District in the Hebei-Shandong-Henan border region, where Zhao remained until 1946. During this period he served as a secretary of the Hua xian CCP Work Committee (where he was involved in land reform during 1945-1946), and director of the CCP Propaganda Department and Organization Department for the Third Special District.[2] Thus very early in his career he was exposed to three key areas of Party work: agriculture, propaganda, and personnel. Other individuals who would later become national leaders and are known to have worked in this border region, and with whom Zhao may have come into contact, were An Ziwen, Xie Fuzhi, Huang Zhen, Li Xuefeng, Liu Bocheng, Bo Yibo, Su Zhenhua, Song Renzhong, Wang Renzhong, and Yang Dezhi. In 1946 Zhao relocated to the Dongboshan mountain region in the Ouyuan base area (also known as the Fourth Rear Base Area) in the Henan-Hebei-Anhui border region, where he continued his work in the Propaganda and Organization Departments.[3] In the Ouyuan base area Zhao served under Li Xiannian, who was the region's commander for the Fourth Front Army. Other important members of the Fourth Front Army with whom Zhao might have had contact were Xu Shiyou, Xu Xiangqian, Chen Xilian, and Liao Chengzhi.[4] In 1948 Zhao was

1

transferred to southwestern Henan where he served as deputy secretary of the Dongbai xian CCP Committee, and then first secretary of the Nanyang District CCP Committee until 1951.

It is not clear exactly when Zhao arrived in Guangdong province. He was first identified there in May 1951 as the assistant director of the South China Sub-Bureau's Land Reform Committee. This date suggests that he arrived in April as part of a large contingent of northern cadres who were sent (by the Central-South Bureau in Wuhan) to enforce a harsher land reform policy than had previously been implemented under the direction of Ye Jianying, Fang Fang, and Li Xuefeng. As Ezra Vogel describes in his classic account, Canton Under Communism, local patronage networks coupled with an official "peaceful land reform" policy in the first year of communist rule, prevented the CCP from penetrating the rural political power structure in Guangdong.[5] At the behest of central political authorities, the "peaceful" land reform policy turned harsh in the winter of 1950-1951, and new personnel from the north were assigned to Guangdong to administer the new policy.[6] The center apparently achieved the desired results. A brutal campaign against landlords and other "bad elements" was carried out during the spring of 1951. Their land was confiscated and redistributed, and many of them were executed. In his capacity as assistant director of the Land Reform Committee, Zhao was involved in overseeing the work teams and personally participated in several "struggle sessions" (douzheng hui) against landlords in the central and northern districts of Guangdong. His "hard line" against all elements of the bourgeoisie put him at odds with Ye Jianying and Fang Fang, who advocated leniency for relatives of overseas Chinese and the petit bourgeoisie.

By August 1951 Zhao had been promoted to secretary-general of the South-China Sub-Bureau Secretariat and had become a member of the Sub-Bureau's Standing Committee.[7] As secretary-general, Zhao worked at the nexus of day-to-day provincial affairs.[8] The secretary-general is the major conduit in the document transmission process from higher to lower authorities, is responsible for briefing the first secretary on these documents, and overseeing the drafting process of the latter's reports and speeches. Thus, as an information manager, Zhao held one of the tools of power in the Chinese political system. Since the Chinese political system is a highly compartmentalized bureaucratic one where directives flow vertically down from the center and local reports upward, Zhao was in the perfect position to keep tabs on local officials and interpret directives to suit his and other's needs.

It is unclear who is to be credited with Zhao's promotion to this position, but it is reasonable to assume that Du Rensheng, in his capacity as secretary-general of the CCP Central-South Bureau, had something to do with it. Like Zhao, Du is also an agricultural specialist and at that time was known to be a leading exponent of harsh land reform policy. Du served concurrently as vice-director (under Li Xuefeng) of the Central-South Land Reform Committee. In 1954 Du was transferred to Beijing, where he continued his work in agricultural affairs. Thus, Zhao and Du had contact early in their careers. Today Zhao and Du continue to work together. In 1982 Zhao (Premier and Director of the State Council's Committee on Restructuring the Economy) appointed Du to head the State Council's Commission on Rural Policy Research.

As secretary-general Zhao delivered an important speech to an enlarged cadre meeting (6-20 August 1951) that was convened at the behest of the Wuhan authorities who were upset over the slow pace of land reform and wanted to affix blame on the appropriate local cadres as a first step towards purging them from their positions. In his speech, Zhao called on low-level cadres to severely criticize all higher-level cadres who obstructed land reform.[9] In so doing, Zhao was following the lead of his superiors in Wuhan, not in the Guangdong Party apparatus (e.g., Ye Jianying and Fang Fang). An outpouring of criticism ensued, the thrust of which however was not against the slow pace of land reform, but rather the harsh tactics practiced by the northerners. This is not what the authorities in Wuhan had in mind. The Central-South Bureau responded with a propaganda campaign that attempted to explain that the harsh policy was necessitated by the Korean War and over one hundred "democratic personages" were dispatched from the center to survey the political landscape.[10] In addition, many more northern cadres were sent down to quell the resistance and speed up land reform, which from the center's perspective continued to lag because of "localism" (difang zhuyi).

The most prominent of these new arrivals was Tao Zhu. Tao would later become the most powerful figure in south China, as well as Zhao's superior and patron, over the next fifteen years. Tao arrived in late January or early February 1952 from Wuhan where he had been a leading official in the Central-South Bureau.[11] One of his first tasks was to conduct a survey of the current status of land reform. Zhao was appointed to oversee the inspection teams.[12] This was the start of their close working relationship.

Tao's major obstacle was Fang Fang. Fang was the titular chairman of the Land Reform Committee and third secretary of the South China Sub-Bureau, ranking just above Tao, the fourth secretary, in the pecking order. In effect, Fang Fang ran the provincial Party apparatus. First secretary Ye Jianying was much more involved in military affairs, and the second secretary, Zhang Yunyi, was in charge of Guangxi province. Fang, a native of Guangdong, spoke a variety of local dialects, and had been an important guerilla leader there before 1949. His contacts and influence thus ranged throughout the province. Fang was not easy to dislodge. Tao's strategy was not to attack him directly and immediately, but rather to isolate him by means of well-timed preemptions on agriculture and land reform policy, and purges of Fang's cronies. Zuo Hongtao was the first to go. Since Zuo had served directly under Zhao as assistant secretary-general of the Sub-Bureau, it is not unlikely that Zhao played a key role in Zuo's purge, although firm evidence to confirm this is lacking. Zuo, along with Yang Qi, another of Fang Fang's cronies, were expelled from the Communist Party on 1 April 1952.[13]

Tao's next step was to attack Fang's followers at the district level. He launched a series of rectification (zhengfeng) campaigns in all Guangdong districts (except Hainan Island). Tao personally directed the campaign in the central district, while Zhao directed it in the northern district. In Zhao's bailiwick, over one thousand cadres were purged.[14] The method of rectification employed was so-called "closed door" group criticism (guanmen piping mi), which was followed by dismissal.[15] As Frederick Teiwes has pointed out, the Guangdong purges were only part of the nation-wide "Three-Anti" and "Five-Anti" rectification campaigns, and tactics varied regionally.[16] In south China, where localism and corruption were most widespread, attacks on cadres were harsh and purges were extensive. In a number of cases, Guangdong included, entire county Party committees were disbanded.[17] Following the local rectification campaign, an enlarged provincial cadre conference was held in late June. Land reform still dominated the agenda of the conference. Tao Zhu presided, and Ye Jianying (still first secretary) gave the keynote speech, in which he praised Tao and Zhao for their leadership in the rectification campaign and apologized for the errors of local cadres.[18] Fang Fang also appeared, urging support for land reform, but offering no apologies for his past behavior.[19] Gu Dacun, another of Fang Fang's close associates dating from Fang's guerilla days and a provincial Party secretary and vice governor, also delivered a speech in which he apologized for the local cadres' ideological deviation.[20] By so doing, Gu was able to separate himself from Fang Fang. This helped Gu avoid being dismissed with Fang the following year, although Gu's time would also come during the Anti-Rightist Campaign.

Gradually, Fang Fang's power base was eroding, and Tao Zhu was the beneficiary. Fang's political allies had either deserted him or been purged, he was no longer the official spokesman on land reform, and his public visibility declined dramatically throughout 1952. In October, he was demoted from third to fifth secretary. Finally, in May 1953 he was forced to confess his "crimes against the people" at a salt workers meeting.[21] Fang's days in Guangdong were over and if it were not for his personal connections (guanxi) his career may well have been over too. But in 1954 Fang appeared in Beijing as Liao Chengzhi's assistant on the Overseas Chinese Affairs Commission, where he finished his career in a largely ceremonial capacity. At any rate, he left Guangdong and concomitantly a major obstacle to Tao's consolidation of power was removed.

The last remaining obstacle to Tao's consolidation of power was Ye Jianying. Ye had a strong local power base, but also had national stature as a People's Liberation Army (PLA) marshal, a Central Committee member, and a ranking member in the Central-South Military Region and Party Bureau. His regional and national positions proved to be a method to remove him from his local posts. In late 1952 and early 1953, Ye began to spend most of his time in Wuhan and then in 1954 in Beijing. No official announcement was made of his departure and change in portfolio, but in May 1953 Tao Zhu was named acting first secretary of the Sub-Bureau (a position he had held de facto since October 1952).[22]

With Tao now in control of the provincial apparatus, Zhao's position became more secure. In September 1953 Zhao was named director of the Rural Work Department, and he continued to serve as secretary-general of the South China Sub-Bureau Secretariat. As director of the Rural Work Department Zhao had An Pingsheng as a deputy. An would go on to become a leading figure in the southwestern provinces of Guangxi and Yunnan. As secretary-general, Zhao continued his aforementioned duties, but was also charged with overseeing the continuing purge of cadres guilty of "localism," corruption, Guomindang ties, and opposition to land reform. The total number of cadres purged was significant; according to official sources, amounting to approximately 71,200 at the county level and above.[23] Zhao, together with Yang Yizhen and Ou Mengjue (the director and vice-director respectively of the CCP Organization Department for the Sub-Bureau), also oversaw the rapid increase in Party recruitment. Between 1949 and the end of 1954, CCP membership in Guangdong increased from 40,000 to 200,000.[24] This increase parallels the rapid Party recruitment nationwide during this period.[25] The need for administrative cadres during this period, coupled with recruitment drives and activists who exhibited their prowess during campaigns, swelled the Party's ranks.

On the whole, Zhao's first three years in Guangdong were ones of establishing his political and professional credentials. During this time Zhao broadened his areas of policy expertise. As was the case in the Ouyuan base area, Zhao was involved in personnel management, one of the keys to political power in China. Not only did he continue to be involved in the rectification and recruitment of cadres, but according to one source, he also taught them mobilization techniques at the Party school in Guangzhou.[26] Zhao's work in the agricultural sphere also continued via his major role in the implementation of land reform. Lastly, he broadened his political base through his central role in the document transmission and drafting process for the Sub-Bureau. His successful work in these three issue areas—agriculture (land reform), personnel management, and information management (document flow), earned him the respect and patronage of Tao Zhu and probably others at the Central-South Bureau in Wuhan. While it is clear that Zhao worked with Tao and others in the provincial Party apparatus, the extent of his contact with officials in the Central-South Bureau in Wuhan such as Li Xiannian, Lin Biao, and Wang Renzhong cannot be documented. Further, there is no evidence that Zhao had any contact during this period with Deng Xiaoping, Deng Zihui or Chen Yun, not to mention such very senior leaders as Mao Zedong, Liu Shaoqi, and Zhou Enlai.

NOTES

1. Donald Klein and Ann Clark, Biographic Dictionary of Chinese Communism, Vol. I (Cambridge, 1971), p. 43. Other biographical sources for Zhao's career used throughout this study include Beijing Review, No. 37 (15 September 1980), p. 4; China Aktuell Supplement, PRC Official Activities (Hamburg, September 1980), p. 40; Union Research Service Biographical Service (hereafter URS), No. 841 (Hong Kong, 7 January 1964); Issues and Studies, Vol. XVI, No. 12 (Taipei, December 1980); "Zhao Ziyang's Record," Ye Zhan Bao (Open Warfare Bulletin), No. 10, 1967, translated in Survey of Mainland China Press (hereafter SCMP), No. 4085 (December 1967), pp. 18-19.

2. Xiandai Zhongguo Renmin Zidian (Tokyo, 1972), p. 644.

3. William Whitson and Chen-hsia Huang, The Chinese High Command (New York, 1973), pp. 80-81, 127, 334-35; Klein and Clark, Biographic Dictionary, Vol. II, p. 1070.

4. See Zhao's biography in the Zhong Gong Ming Lu (Taipei, revised ed., 1978), pp. 87-88.

5. Ezra Vogel, Canton Under Communism (Cambridge, 2d ed., 1980). On pp. 95-121, Vogel depicts in great detail the evolution of land reform in Guangdong.

6. Enunciated by Teng Zihui in a major speech in Wuhan in January 1951. See Current Background (hereafter CB), No. 227, 8 January 1951. For more on "peaceful land reform," see Vivienne Shue, Peasant China in Transition (Berkeley, 1980), pp. 82-85; Thomas Bernstein, Leadership and Mobilization in the Collectivization of Agriculture in China and Russia: A Comparison (Ph.D. dissertation, Columbia University, 1970), ch. III.

7. Evidence of Zhao's appointment can be found in Nanfang Ribao (hereafter NFRB), 5 September 1951; Vogel, Canton Under Communism, p. 390 (n. 64) where Zhao is described as an "ardent leftist," presumably referring only to his "radical" (i.e., harsh) actions in land reform.

8. For a description of the duties of the secretary-general, see A. Doak Barnett, Cadres, Bureaucracy and Political Power in Communist China (New York, 1967), pp. 135-36; and Kenneth Lieberthal, Central Documents and Politburo Politics (Ann Arbor, 1978), ch. III ("Central Documents: The Transmission Process").

9. NFRB, 5 September 1951.

10. Vogel, Canton Under Communism, p. 116.

11. Klein and Clark, Biographic Dictionary, Vol. II, p. 810.

12. NFRB, 5 and 10 February 1952.

13. Vogel, Canton Under Communism, p. 118.

14. NFRB, 22 April 1952; Gong Shan Ribao (Hong Kong), 2 May 1952.

15. Frederick Teiwes, Politics and Purges in China: Rectification and the Decline of Party Norms, 1950-1965 (White Plains, 1979); see particularly ch. 2, on the rectification process, and ch. 4, on the 1950-1953 period.

16. Ibid., pp. 105-66. For a different perspective on rural rectification during this period, which equates rectification with the "mass line" (thus ignoring its coercive nature), see Shue, Peasant China in Transition, pp. 36-40.

17. NFRB, 9 May 1952.

18. Vogel, Canton Under Communism, pp. 118-19; NFRB, 12 July 1952; CB, No. 211 (1952).

19. CB, ibid.

20. Vogel, Canton Under Communism, p. 119; NFRB, 24 July 1952; CB, ibid.

21. NFRB, 29 May 1953. His "crimes" included closing salt mines which put 130,000 workers out of work, not allowing the masses to sell commodities in order to buy goods for New Year's, and alienating intellectuals by persecuting teachers during the rectification campaign. See Vogel, Canton Under Communism, p. 120.

22. Klein and Clark, Biographic Dictionary, Vol. II, p. 810; Vogel, Canton Under Communism, p. 119; NFRB, 17 May 1953; CB, No. 226; Peter R. Moody, Jr., "Policy and Power: The Career of Tao Zhu, 1956-66," in China Quarterly, No. 54 (1973).

23. This figure is derived from NFRB's estimate of 89,000 as of 13 December 1953, and is then divided by .80 because NFRB announced on 9 December 1957 that eighty percent of local cadres at county level and above had lost their positions in the wake of land reform. There is no way of estimating how many of the claimed 100,000 sub-county level cadres were purged. See Vogel, Canton Under Communism, pp. 121, 391 (n. 106), 371 (Table 3).

24. Vogel, Canton Under Communism, p. 371 (Table 4).

25. See for example Ying-mao Kau, "Patterns of Recruitment and Mobility of Urban Cadres," in John Wilson Lewis (Ed.), The City in Communist China (Stanford, 1971), pp. 97-121; Franz Schurmann, Ideology and Organization in Communist China (Berkeley, 2d ed., 1966), pp. 167-72; and Heath B. Chamberlain, "Transition and Consolidation in Urban China: A Study of Leaders and Organizations in Three Cities, 1949-53," in Robert Scalapino (Ed.), Elites in the People's Republic of China (Seattle, 1972), pp. 245-301.

26. Zhong Gong Ming Lu (Taipei, 1978), p. 87.

2
Campaigns and Career
Advancement, 1954–1960

The seven years between the end of land reform (1953) and the end of the Great Leap Forward (1960) were ones of alternating economic mobilization and retrenchment, culminating in the debacle of the Great Leap Forward. The period was punctuated by numerous campaigns for both political and economic purposes. Many a career was made through the proper administration of, and zealous participation in, these campaigns. Zhao's career was no exception. During this period Zhao's personal policy preferences (especially in agriculture) became clear and his political instinct became honed. His official positions and job responsibilities multiplied rapidly during this period. The following is a descriptioin of his official positions and responsibilities during this period.

Zhao continued as director of the Rural Work Department until 1955, but relinquished his post as secretary-general of the South China Sub-Bureau Secretariat in 1954 when he assumed new positions. In July 1954 Zhao represented the central district of Guangdong at the first provincial People's Congress[1] (part of a nationwide attempt by the regime to strengthen local government).[2] In October 1954 he was identified as third secretary of the South China Sub-Bureau,[3] a position he held until the Sub-Bureau was abolished in July 1955. In November 1954 Zhao was appointed as the "general commander" of the Guangdong "Headquarters for Grain Procurement."[4] In February 1955 he was elected to the Guangdong People's Congress, where he served on the Presidium.[5] In July 1955 Zhao was named deputy secretary of the provincial CCP Secretariat, a position he occupied until November 1956.[6] In August 1955 Zhao was identified as chairman of the Sub-Tropical Resources Development Committee, which was charged with overseeing resource exploitation on Hainan Island and other special Guangdong districts.[7] The only new position in which Zhao was identified in 1956 is first political commissar of the Guangdong Military District (MD).[8] In April 1957 Zhao was promoted to general secretary of the Secretariat of the provincial CCP committee, thus regaining the position he had held in the Sub-Bureau.[9] In November 1957 he was identified as secretary of the Guangdong CCP Military District Committee.[10] Zhao assumed no new posts between 1958 and 1961.

As director of the Rural Work Department, Zhao was responsible for promoting the Party's numerous programs in the countryside and for directing the activities of all government agencies in the fields of agriculture, forestry, water conservancy, land reclamation, and veterinary medicine.[11] Needless to say, these were not small tasks. Everything from running campaigns to directing large-scale irrigation and land reclamation projects fell within his purview. As chief of the province's Grain Procurement Bureau, Zhao was charged with the sensitive and difficult tasks of monitoring output, enforcing quotas and taxes, and ensuring distribution.

As third secretary of the Sub-Bureau, Zhao's main duty was management of a functional issue area (in his case, agriculture) and keeping the first secretary (Tao Zhu) informed of all related developments in this area. He was responsible for "signing-off" on all agriculture-related documents, ensuring that directives were properly implemented, drafting reports and speeches for the first secretary, and generally being at his disposal. As such, Zhao would often appear with Tao, or in his place, when high-ranking leaders or foreigners passed through Guangzhou. On 30 June 1954, for example, he met Zhou Enlai at the airport (this is the first reported meeting between the two men).[12] During this period he also met with officials from Poland, the Japanese Communist Party, East Germany, North Vietnam, the Ceylonese Communist Party, and Burma.[13]

As first political commissar of the Guangdong MD, Zhao's main responsibility was to oversee the ideological indoctrination (i.e., the dissemination of current Party policy) of PLA troops in the province. As such, he worked closely with the PLA's General Political Department (GPD), one of the three principle staff components of the PLA after the 1954 reorganization.[14]

Finally, as deputy secretary and then full secretary-general of the Secretariat of the provincial CCP Committee, Zhao sat at the very center of political power in the province. There are many sources of power in the Chinese political system; knowledge is one of them, and information comprises knowledge. The Secretariat is the nerve center of the information and document transmission system in the CCP. As deputy secretary, Zhao was in charge of all documents relating to his functional area of agriculture, but as secretary-general his bailiwick extended to all five functional systems (<u>xitong</u>): rural work, political and legal affairs, propaganda and education, industry and communication, and finance and trade. The authority inherent in this position is not to be underestimated. Tao Zhu was largely dependent on the information Zhao provided him. Zhao was in charge of receiving, interpreting (in spirit or to the letter), and disseminating central directives (zhongfa).[15] If a document required redrafting, this too was his job to coordinate. Furthermore, he was responsible for organizing reference materials and the drafting of the "work report" (in effect, the agenda) to be given by the leading cadre at provincial "work conferences" where policy options are considered and made before being presented to higher organs for pro forma adoption.[16] He was also responsible for overseeing the drafting of Tao Zhu's major reports and speeches.[17] As secretary-general of the Secretariat, Zhao's counterpart at the center was none other than Deng Xiaoping. This is the first instance when the two had a clear opportunity to come into contact, but specific evidence of such contact is lacking. Given the bureaucratic chain of command, however, it is reasonable to assume that they worked together. Lastly, Zhao's duties as secretary-general also included being the ultimate editor-in-chief of the provincial CCP bi-monthly journal Shangyu.[18] In a society where news is controlled and the media is a major instrument of propaganda and policy dissemination, Zhao's potential influence in this realm was substantial. In short, while Zhao was not the highest ranking official in Guangdong, he may have been the most powerful, if one considers the levers of political power that he controlled or to which he had access.

The main trend in the appearance data for Zhao during 1954-1960 is that agriculture-related policy issues dominated his time. Consequently, the following discussion will focus on Guangdong's agricultural development during this period, and we will attempt to depict Zhao's involvement in this issue area.

In late 1953, Zhao's first year as director of the Rural Work Department, the central government announced the policy of "compulsory buying and selling of grain." What this meant was that in addition to paying a grain tax (established in 1950), peasants also had to meet output quotas and sell their grain to the state at artificially low prices.[19] The government in turn sold it back to the populace in state stores at fixed low prices. Because of tardy land reform and continuing localism in Guangdong, this program was actually introduced six months later than in other locales.[20] When it was introduced in 1954, the burden of explanation and enforcement fell upon Zhao and his Rural Work Department.

These were not easy tasks. Compliance was only partial, and hoarding was frequent. The reasons for this were as follows. First, peasants were simply not willing to sell the bulk of their produce for an artificially low return and no profit. Second, after the harsh land reform many were wary of CCP intrusion into their lives. Third, in 1953 grain was not plentiful in the province; Guangdong was still a net importer of grain. Total output had in fact dropped by almost one billion catties from 1952 to 1953 (18.9 to 17.8).[21] Against this backdrop Zhao was named to the sensitive position of director ("general commander") of the newly-created Grain Procurement Bureau in November 1954. He got immediate results. Total output increased twenty percent to 21 billion catties in 1954.[22] The center had criticized the province for poor grain collections in the spring harvest, thus extra efforts were made after the fall harvest. Usually sixty percent of the annual state collections come from the fall harvest, but in 1954 over seventy percent of the annual quotas were fulfilled after this harvest.[23] The effects of this windfall collection in 1954 were increased hoarding, underreporting of output in the spring of 1955, and a shortage of cash crops being planted. The result was a ten percent drop in output for the spring 1955 harvest.[24]

The government responded with the "Three Fix Campaign" (sanding yundong). This campaign was a modification of the aforementioned "buying and selling" policy (two of the "three fixes"), designed to reduce peasant resistance to quotas by tying them to production (the third "fix"). That is, instead of the peasant having to sell a set amount of grain to the state (based on his relative contribution of land, tools, and animals), his quota was now fixed in proportion to his production. Moreover, the overall provincial quota was reduced for 1955. It was hoped that lower quotas, along with directives not to extract production beyond quotas, would induce peasants to plant more cash crops in order to supplement their income and increase the variety of vegetables for urban markets. Another aim of the campaign was to gather accurate statistics on the costs and factors of production. The government simply did not know the labor-power and productive capacity of Guangdong's six million rural households, and therefore could not fairly fix quotas.

The "Three Fix Campaign" was administered by the Rural Work Department (under Zhao's control). Work teams were sent down to the basic levels from special district and county offices, but as many as two thousand work teams were sent from provincial and municipal government, Party, and army offices.[25] These teams gathered information on production, the previous years' sales and purchases, and the general standard of living in the area. This information was vital to planners preparing for accelerated collectivization.

At the very time when the work teams were in the countryside, Mao and the Central Committee in Beijing were arguing over whether to accelerate the pace of collectivization. On one side of the debate was Mao, who wanted to accelerate collectivization. On the other side were those who preferred a more gradual policy. The latter group included Liu Shaoqi, Chen Yun, and Deng Zihui (Director of the Rural Work Department).[26] Mao ultimately won the debate, which meant that all existing mutual aid teams (MATs) and experimental ("lower") agricultural producers' cooperatives (APCs) would be amalgamated and expanded into "higher" APCs. The

Central Committee announced that 32,000 APCs were to be established in Guangdong by the spring of 1956.[27] This figure was readjusted upward to 45,000 after Mao's famous speech of 31 July to a conference of provincial secretaries.[28] Mao called this conference in an effort to circumvent his opponents at the center by appealing directly to provincial authorities on whom he could rely (a tactic he used frequently in his career).[29] In his capacity as a ranking provincial secretary (responsible for agriculture) and Director of the Rural Work Department, Zhao should have attended the meeting. All of the available appearance data indicate that he did not. Taken together with the fact that Zhao had made only one public appearance since February, this may be the first indication of Zhao's reluctance to embrace accelerated collectivization of agriculture. After Mao's speech, the Guangdong provincial CCP Committee convened an Enlarged Cadre Work Conference in August to work out the details of the new policy.[30] Again Zhao was not listed as having attended. This is especially strange given his position as the leading provincial official in charge of agriculture. His absence from these conferences is empirically inexplicable; one can only conjecture that he opposed the trend toward accelerated collectivization. At this conference, provincial cadres who had opposed early collectivization efforts were denounced as "rightists" (Zhao was not among them), and a new directive on cooperatives was drafted. This document was adopted in September at a provincial Party Congress. The new targets were set at 70,000 cooperatives to be established by the spring of 1956 and 125,000 by the fall of 1957.[31] All subprovincial levels (county, district, township) were assigned quotas. After the Sixth Plenum of the Seventh Central Committee met from 4 to 11 October in Beijing (where Mao criticized Deng Zihui), there was yet another call for acceleration. In November another special conference of cadres from province, district, and county levels was convened.[32] The target for the spring of 1956 was increased to 85,000.[33] The work teams were sent down again en masse, and the target was met early, when the provincial government proclaimed at the end of January 1956 that 132,304 cooperatives had been formed, with eighty percent of rural households participating.[34] By the end of February, half of these were higher APCs, and by the fall all of rural Guangdong was organized into these collectives.[35]

From the center's perspective, the "high tide" had ebbed and rural "socialist transformation" had been accomplished. Mao had been vindicated. The Chairman maintained his political initiative by convening yet another conference of like-minded provincial secretaries (from which Zhao was again absent) in Tianjin in November 1955, where a draft of the "Twelve Year National Program for the Development of Agriculture" was written.[36] This document was revised at a Politburo meeting in January 1956 and dubbed the "Forty Points on Agriculture."[37] It was submitted later that month to a Supreme State Conference for adoption.[38] The document called for a continuation of the fairly radical line advanced by Mao since the previous summer and established a number of very ambitious agricultural output targets and socio-economic goals.[39] The method employed to attain these targets and goals was the mass mobilization of labor. In Guangdong, Tao Zhu endorsed this ambitious document at a provincial Chinese People's Political Consultative Conference (CPPCC) meeting in February and in fact stated that all goals set forth in the "Forty Points" would be achieved in Guangdong by 1962, five years ahead of schedule![40] Though Zhao is known to have attended this meeting, there is no indication that he spoke or publicly endorsed the program.[41] If Zhao was reluctant about the Chairman's program, he was not alone.

The so-called "moderates" in the central leadership launched a counterattack against Mao and his program in the spring of 1956. To be sure, Khrushchev's denunciation of Stalin in February had given them added impetus, especially with respect to the personality cult issue. An indication that the counterattack was underway came when the Seventh Plenum failed to convene as scheduled on 1 April, and therefore failed to adopt the "Forty Points" as official policy (which had been anticipated). Throughout the spring the national press attacked various elements of the First Five Year Plan and the Forty Points. "Moderate" leaders (Zhou Enlai, Chen Yun, Guo Moruo, Bo Yibo, Peng Zhen, Deng Zihui, Li Fuchun, and others) articulated these complaints and put forth revised policies at the National People's Congress (NPC) in June.[42] More emphasis was placed on supporting light industry, increasing material incentives, improving living standards, supporting intellectuals, making use of the bourgeois capitalists' expertise, etc. For his part, Deng Zihui attacked the mismanagement of APCs, the use of coercion, unrealistic targets, etc. By the time the Seventh Plenum of the Seventh Central Committee finally met in August, the Forty Points had clearly been shelved, if not killed, and Mao was on the defensive. The stage was set for the events of the Eighth Party Congress in September--the "moderates' " heyday.

The Eighth Party Congress reiterated and elaborated the policies articulated at the June NPC. With regard to agriculture, a joint Party-government directive was issued on the eve of the Party Congress which in effect replaced the Forty Points. It advocated, for the first time, the adoption of the "three freedoms" (sanzi) of increased private plots, rural trade fairs ("free markets"), and sideline production for peasants.[43] The Eighth Congress also marked an increase in Tao Zhu's power as he was made a member of the Central Committee.

After two random appearances in early 1956, Zhao continued to be largely absent from public view during the summer and fall.[44] His only appearance was at a provincial Party Congress in August.[45] This absence during most of the year remains inexplicable. We can only surmise that he was either ill (physically or politically), on a prolonged rural inspection tour, or that his job as deputy secretary of the provincial CCP Secretariat (July 1955-November 1956) did not require maintaining a public posture.

Whatever the explanation for his notable absences, Zhao began to appear regularly again in 1957. In February he delivered the closing address to a provincial cadres conference on APCs.[46] The Guangdong leadership's choice of Zhao to deliver this speech marked his return to the public political stage and may have been an indication of his pending promotion to secretary-general of the Guangdong CCP Secretariat in April. In March Zhao's next task was to oversee a rectification campaign in which 80,000 cadres were sent to the countryside to live and work with peasants and receive their criticism.[47] This campaign was intended to compensate the peasants for the excesses of the previous year's campaign against counterrevolutionaries (sufan yundong) while simultaneously preparing for the Hundred Flowers rectification campaign in May. This rectification campaign was to be different than past ones. This was to be "open-door" rectification, i.e., non-Party members were permitted to criticize cadres. All areas of Party and government policy and behavior since 1949 were fair game for criticism. The regime felt secure enough to entertain such criticism and hoped to use the campaign to coopt wavering elements. Liu Shaoqi visited Guangzhou on 10 April to brief Tao, Zhao, Ou Mengjue, and other local leaders on the aims and administration of this "great blooming and contending" campaign.[48] This was probably the first time Zhao met Liu. Following Liu's visit, the provincial committee met and decided to dispatch leading officials to various provincial districts, where they were to brief local Party cadres on the goals of the campaign, minimize Party resistance to public criticism, assure the "masses" that the request for criticism was genuine, and personally receive criticism.[49] Zhao, Ou Mengjue, Feng Baiju, Li Jianzhen, and others were dispatched to the countryside for these purposes. After initial hesitancy, an immense outpouring of criticism ensued from all quarters. While Zhao personally emerged relatively unscathed, a number of policies with which he had been associated were sharply attacked. Land reform and the sufan campaign were criticized for their brutality; collectivization was criticized for its hastiness and ill-consideration of local conditions; the supply of agricultural produce was criticized for being meager; the setting of prices and quotas were criticized as being too high and compensation too low.[50] Dissatisfaction with rural conditions in general, and the cooperatives in particular, was so great that the provincial government revealed that a total of 117,916 households had pulled out of the cooperatives during the spring.[51] These are only the criticisms pertaining to agriculture, while in fact they extended to practically every realm of government policy.[52]

The central leadership was taken aback by the nationwide outpouring of criticism (although some argue that it was merely a trap laid by Mao, especially the last thirteen days) and put an abrupt end to the "blooming and contending" (which had lasted only five weeks) on 8 June 1957. With a sharply worded editorial in the People's Daily titled "What Is This For?" the Anti-Rightist Campaign was launched. As the campaign unfolded throughout the summer, intellectuals, "Democratic Party" personages, former capitalists, and remaining landlords were "capped" with a "rightist" label with which they would have to live for the next twenty years. Their disillusion, humiliation, and other psychological pressures precipitated by the mass "struggle sessions" drove many to suicide. Many of those who survived were stripped of their positions and possessions and sent to rural labor camps (where many remained for more than twenty years).

Zhao's role in the Anti-Rightist Campaign remains unclear. He was not reported in the press as making any public appearances between early May (when he toured various district Party committees to propagate the rectification campaign) and 25 July, when he appeared at a provincial Party congress.[53] He then disappeared from public view again until November, when he delivered a report to the Second CCP Congress of the Guangdong Military District.[54] To be sure, his position as secretary-general was not a high-visibility post; his main job was to process documents. It is reasonable to assume that during this time Zhao was involved in administering the Rural Socialist Education Movement which began in mid-summer and continued through October. This campaign was the rural counterpart to the predominantly urban Anti-Rightist Campaign. The intent of the leadership and Mao, who personally launched it at the Qingdao work conference in July, was that this was primarily to be an ideological campaign, administered by work teams, and aimed at propagating the comparative virtues of socialist and capitalist agriculture, i.e., the "two road" debate.[55] In reality, however, at least in Guangdong, the campaign became an effort to mobilize the peasantry for productive purposes: getting in the harvest, meeting state grain quotas, and planting the winter crop.[56] Intellectuals and students who were sent to the countryside to help launch the campaign soon discovered that much of their work was in the fields.[57] The distortion of the campaign for the purpose of maintaining production is a characteristic which Zhao repeatedly demonstrates throughout his career. This is just one instance. Other evidence which suggests Zhao's involvement in this campaign is that he gave a keynote speech on "current rural conditions" at the end of the campaign at a provincial Party congress on 21 November.[58] In this speech, Zhao took both cadres and some peasants to task:

> Some cadres do not have confidence in the majority of the masses
> . . . . In the countryside the most reliable forces are the poor and

> lower middle peasants. . . . Rich and middle peasants outside coop-
> eratives take advantage of the slackness in management . . . to
> engage in private business, to speculate, to avoid taxes, to ruin the
> state's market management. . . . This attracts unstable co-op mem-
> bers to leave the co-ops and go on their own.[59]

While this congress marked the end of the Rural Socialist Education Movement, it also kicked off another campaign against "localism" (difang zhuyi). This campaign lasted until May 1958, and its main casualties were two leading provincial officials, both of whom were nominally Zhao's superiors: Gu Dacun and Feng Baiju. Both men were ranking provincial secretaries, vice governors, and alternate members of the Central Committee. Both were natives of Guangdong and had spent their entire careers there. Both had been famous guerilla leaders before 1949 and had built strong power bases in their respective districts: Feng on Hainan Island and Gu in the East River area. Because Feng was particularly well-entrenched he was able to block the implementation of numerous policies, ordered by higher authorities, with which he disagreed.[60] Ou Mengjue (director of the Guangdong CCP Organization Department) wrote a long article at the time of their purge detailing their "crimes and deviations."[61] Feng was accused of everything from blocking land reform to instigating a "miniature Hungarian incident" (i.e., a revolt) in a northern Hainan district in the spring of 1957.[62] Gu was also accused of blocking land reform, being "an extreme individualist and right opportunist," and having formed an "anti-Party clique" with Feng.[63] However, in view of their "long revolutionary history," Ou concluded, both men should be able to retain their Party membership while being relieved "of their more important posts."[64] With this caveat, their eclipse was short-lived. Both returned to Guangdong provincial posts within a year, although their official and actual power were greatly diminished. Shortly thereafter, Feng was transferred to Zhejiang province. Both finished out their careers effectively stripped of power.

The purges of Fang and Gu opened the way for Zhao to advance even further. Zhao, now working directly under Tao Zhu, immediately acquired a higher public profile.[65] His main responsibilities over the next few years continued to be in the agricultural sector, on which topic he authored a number of articles, made numerous speeches, and led many inspection tours in the countryside. This, of course, was the period of the Great Leap Forward and the formation of people's communes (renmin gongshe). We will attempt to trace Zhao's involvement in these epic events as they unfolded in Guangdong.

The years 1956 and 1957 had not been good ones for the Guangdong economy. Agricultural production was stagnant, and grain shortages existed throughout the province. Thus the primary focus of the provincial Party congress of November-December 1957 was grain output for 1958. The congress approved a local version of Mao's "Thirty-Six Articles" on agriculture, which called for a 6.1 percent increase in output for 1958. This figure was 1.4 percent greater than the recommended national figure and, though herculean, it was still modest compared to later goals.[66] Immediately following the congress, Tao Zhu and Zhao led provincial Party officials on a forty-day inspection tour of the winter crop.[67] They returned convinced of the potential for a "great leap forward" in agricultural output, a prognosis they would later have cause to regret and criticize. Upon their return from the tour in January, Tao and Zhao called for quadrupling the target for 1958, to 800 catties per mu.[68] Zhao was given the task of breaking this news to xian-level cadres in a telephone conference in February 1958.[69] Also in February, Zhao and other leaders (Tao Zhu, Chen Yu, Wen Mingsheng, Li Jianzhen, and Ou Mengjue) established an "experimental farm" in the provincial Party committee's model county, Banyou xian.[70] Chairman Mao, on a national mobilization tour, visited this farm on 30 April.[71] This was probably the first time that Zhao met the Chairman. Also in April, another group of high officials including Liu Shaoqi, Deng Xiaoping, Kang Sheng, and Lu Dingyi, visited Guangzhou for an agricultural implements exhibition.[72] Thus, by this time, Zhao had met most of the key central leaders.

By February 1958 and the Second Plenum of the CCP-CC in May, the Great Leap Forward was underway. Zhao was an early supporter of the campaign. He briefed county- and district-level cadres of the Rural Work Department on the new output targets at a meeting in Sunwei in April, and he was a member of the "agricultural inspection corps" who were to "make their way deep into every xian and APC to transmit the spirit of the Congress."[73] He also wrote an article titled "The Pace of Grain Production Can Be Accelerated" for the People's Daily. Zhao's words mirror the optimism of the time:

> Is it possible to speed up grain production in accordance with the "more, faster, better, and more economical" requirement? Experiences gained in Guangdong over the past years, especially last winter and spring, indicate that it is. . . . Barring particularly heavy natural calamities, Guangdong will attain, if not exceed, an annual production increase of six billion catties of grains. We estimate that the province will produce next year, or the one after next at the latest, forty-eight billion catties of grains, laying a reliable foundation for the realization of the provisions of the Agricultural Development Program. . . . What measures have we taken to achieve the target of eight hundred catties of grains per mu?

Improvement in the tilling system and expansion of multi-crop cultivation are the principle roads we have travelled. . . . To ensure rapid progress in grain production, though, we must place the problem of early mechanization on the agenda of the provincial Party committee. Some have thought in the past that the southern part of our country, abundant in paddy fields, is not fit for mechanization and that since the south is full of people for whom there is not adequate land, there is no rush to realize mechanization there. This idea is wrong. . . . Tractors can be used on paddy fields and the masses want early mechanization. . . . Our estimate is that APCs can accumulate enough to buy machines and that the technological conditions in Guangdong are adequate for agricultural mechanization at an early date. It is entirely possible for Guangdong to realize basic mechanization or semi-mechanization within, say, three to five years.[74]

Zhao had clearly caught the optimistic spirit of the Great Leap. He wrote about mass mobilization being the main instrument to achieve production goals, but discussed the need for "redness and expertise" (youhong youzhuan) among cadres: "Persons who are proficient but not red have, in fact, no soul and are bound to lose themselves in the end. At the same time, we feel that persons who claim to be red but are ignorant of the actual conditions are, in fact, falsely red; such persons have no right to make decisions on production and cannot be expected to lead production."[75] This article also marks the beginning of Zhao's publishing career. Between 1958 and 1960 he published eleven articles on agriculture, the majority dealing with raising agricultural output.[76] Since many of these articles were reprinted in the national press, this provided Zhao with national exposure and recognition for the first time.

Following the publication of this article, Zhao disappeared from public view until 1959. During the fall of 1958 Tao Zhu also disappeared from public view. This, of course, was the period of the formation of people's communes, a very odd time indeed for these two men to disappear. Their only public role during the fall was in the print media; each one published an article.[77] Tao's last appearance was at the enlarged Politburo meeting at Beidaihe in August, which kicked off the commune movement, and he did not appear again until the Sixth Plenum in Wuchang (one of the Wuhan tri-cities) in December, which met to scale back the commune movement and readjust targets. Zhao had not been reported in public since the May inspection tour, and he did not appear again until 3 December (while Tao was still in Wuchang), when he presided over a telephone conference of provincial cadres on commune readjustment.[78] The obvious question arising from their public absences is what role the two men played, if any, in the introduction of communes in Guangdong. Is their absence to be construed as opposition to the communes? Given their statements and increased activity in 1959 after the Sixth Plenum's decision to curtail the movement, this is a reasonable conclusion. Anne Thurston arrives at a somewhat different conclusion. She argues that because of the ambiguity of the initial directives, Tao and Zhao were "confused" about the extent of implementation of the movement (the xian versus the qu), and preferred to see how the movement unfolded in other provinces before committing themselves.[79] By so doing, she argues, they were able to emerge relatively unscathed when the leadership backtracked. When Tao and Zhao reappeared, they criticized the "methods of work" of basic-level cadres who had overzealously implemented the movement, thereby alienating many peasants.[80] Consequently, Tao and Zhao opportunistically capitalized on the reverse in policy.

Retrenchment began immediately after the Sixth Plenum and continued until the fall of 1959. In fact, it is correct to say that retrenchment in Guangdong began during the Sixth Plenum when Zhao convened a telephone conference of provincial cadres in February. During this meeting Zhao provided a good sense of his views on communes when he directed that communes were to remain socialist, not communist, i.e., that goods were to be distributed on the basis of labor instead of need. He scolded cadres for working peasants to exhaustion and confiscating their personal property. He further directed the cadres to reassure the masses that their personal property and savings would remain privately owned, that everyone be guaranteed eight hours of sleep and four hours for meals daily. Zhao ordered that these meals should be served hot and in mess halls. The mess halls themselves, which had proven to be the source of much discontent, were placed under production team management so as to be more responsive to local needs. Zhao further ordered the mess halls to be "self-reliant" in livestock and vegetable raising. The commune and production brigade were under strict orders not to commandeer mess hall plots and fixed capital. Lastly, Zhao directed the cadres to help the populace solve the problems of shortages of timber, firewood, coal, pork, and secondary food supplies.[81]

These supply shortages were already bad, but would only get worse. The extravagant quotas and inflated production figures of 1958 had given a false sense of surplus to officials and commoners alike. Virtually every basic consumer good (not the least of which was grain) and raw material was in short supply. The transport delivery system had broken down and people began to hoard what they could. What was to be done?

After returning from the Wuchang Plenum, Tao Zhu made an inspection tour of Dongguan xian in southern Guangdong. Tao's report on Xumen commune was published in the People's Daily.[82] Tao criticized the communes for having been established too rapidly and said that this had caused "departmentalism," which in turn was causing corruption among cadres. In February, the Third Session of the First Guangdong CCP Congress met in Guangzhou. Lin Biao and Ye Jianying attended (probably because they were vacationing in the south and wanted to combine business with pleasure). Zhao delivered a major speech at the congress on "agricultural questions." His focus was on the "Tidying up the Communes" campaign which entailed promoting the "scientific spirit" in agriculture, accelerating grain production, eliminating grain hoarding, and "seeking truth from facts."[83] Mao apparently read Zhao's report. At a May 1959 meeting on Party work style the Chairman discussed a report Zhao had written on commune management and is reported to have said, "The commune problem is very obvious. At what level they should be managed was not made clear last year. . . . I later read the report of Zhao Ziyang."[84] Zhao's report resulted from an inspection tour he had made in January to Xuwen xian in southern Guangdong. Zhao's tour was aimed at ferreting out grain hoarders, since he was convinced that the autumn 1958 harvest had been a bumper one. Zhao consequently launched several anti-grain concealment drives which resulted in numerous purges, suicides, and criticisms of local-level cadres.[85] Mao vehemently disagreed with Zhao's and Tao's perceptions of "departmentalism" and grain concealment, and criticized them at the second Zhengzhou work conference.[86]

Soon after the the Third Session of the First Guangdong CCP congress, as spring planting was getting underway, Zhao gave an interview to Zhongguo Qingnian Bao (China Youth Daily), in which he extolled the virtues of close planting.[87] Zhao claimed that close planting techniques had enabled Guangdong to double its late rice output in 1958. Zhao reiterated his emphasis on the importance of close planting, double cropping, and the use of night soil fertilizer in a June article in the People's Daily.[88]

In May the provincial CCP committee convened a work conference at Shantou. Tao Zhu criticized the Great Leap Forward policies, and came very close to criticizing Mao himself, in his famous speech "The Brilliance of the Sun":

> Everyone knows that sincere treatment of mistakes and defects in work, and sincere inner-Party criticism and self-criticism are impor-tant marks of a Marxist-Leninist political party. I think that to use the metaphor of the brilliance of the sun to describe the leadership of our Party is proper and no exaggeration. . . . But the sun also has blackspots. Some comrades do not like to hear about mistakes and defects.[89]

Zhao also addressed the conference and blamed the "commandism" inherent in commune management as the greatest impediment to instituting the "technical reforms" necessary to increase output. "If the majority of the masses do not agree (with the new policies) we must wait, and under no circumstances may we resort to the simple method of administrative fiat."[90] The work conference concluded that all leading provincial cadres should devote increased time and attention to agricultural matters; Tao Zhu pledged half-time.[91]

Whatever the intentions of the leaders, no policy could cope with nature. As soon as the conference adjourned the heavens opened. Throughout May and the first ten days of June, Guangdong experienced some of its heaviest rains in history, just at the peak of the spring harvest. Dikes broke, fields were flooded, people were stranded from their homes, disease spread, and massive emergency rescue missions were required. Official estimates of destruction claimed that 200,000 homes and 5,000,000 mu of farmland were ruined.[92]

Against this backdrop, several central and provincial leaders, including Tao Zhu and Wang Renzhong of Hubei, continued to criticize the Great Leap. Tao wrote in a People's Daily article, for example: "In 1958 it was necessary to stress our subjective potential, but now we need to give more attention to objective factors, lest we fall into left deviation. In 1957 we went too slow, fearing reckless advance. But in 1958 we went too fast, ignoring the objective laws governing the rate of speed."[93] This article was published just a week before the famous Lushan Plenum convened,[94] and obviously positioned Tao (and probably Zhao) with those who criticized the Chairman and the Great Leap at the conference. The most notable critic was, of course, Defense Minister Peng Dehuai who expressed his sentiments in the "Letter of Opinion" to Mao.[95] The story of Mao's furor and criticism of Peng,[96] Peng's self-criticism at the subsequent Eighth Plenum,[97] and his purge[98] are well known. Following Lushan, a national campaign against "right opportunism" was launched and the Great Leap was revived. What did Tao and Zhao do? They lay low again and appeared infrequently throughout the fall. Zhao's only reported appearance was at the provincial People's Congress which coincided with National Day and the Tenth Anniversary of the People's Republic of China (PRC) in October. Zhao delivered a speech at the Congress in which he bluntly stated his views on the Great Leap.

Some comrades are beginning to be affected by blind optimism and self-complacency. . . . They are even reluctant to face shortcomings; they are willing to listen to what is good but not what is bad. Some comrades are seemingly enthusiastic, but lack a realistic attitude towards work. They talk of targets and plans without adopting serious measures for this achievement and organizing action. They do not carry out supervision and inspection. Much is talked about but little is done. Targets, plans, and output figures exist only on paper. In a situation where the enthusiasm is high, some comrades tend to adopt the work style of over-simplification. The decisions they make are rash. . . . It is necessary to establish the work style of seeking truth from facts and paying close attention to scientific analysis (emphasis added).[99]

Tao was somewhat more active publicly after the congress, as his position mandated, but still kept a lower profile than usual.

Following the fall harvest, the acute grain shortage became apparent to the leadership and the Great Leap was, in effect, abandoned.[100] It was not merely a question of shortages and supply imbalances; actual famine conditions existed in several provinces. Malnutrition existed at a minimum, starvation at a maximum. Tao and Zhao moved back into the limelight and began to attack the problem by decentralizing commune administration via the "four fixes" campaign, ensuring supply via the "three guarantees and one reward" policy, and increasing production via the "three freedoms and one contract" policy. All of these programs were implemented simultaneously in the spring of 1960. The "four fixes" campaign (siguding) assigned land, labor, farm implements, and draft animals to the production team, thus concentrating these factors of production at the lowest—and most useful—level of ownership possible. The "three guarantees and one reward" policy (sanbao yijiang) was a corollary to the "four fixes" in that teams guaranteed a certain amount of costs, workdays, and output to the brigade in return for financial stipends (often received in kind) for those which met their quotas. The effect of these policies was to provide the team with more autonomy in determining exactly how it went about meeting its quotas. This leeway was further extended by the readoption of the "three freedoms and one contract" (sanzi yibao) policy in which private plots, private sideline production, and private "free" markets were encouraged, and output quotas were contracted with the household (baochan daohu). Taken together, these policies formed the heart of the agricultural recovery program promulgated as the "Sixty Articles on Agriculture" (Nongcun renmin gongshe gongzuo tiaoli cao'an) in May 1961, following a central work conference convened in Guangzhou. It is important to note, however, that they were implemented a full year earlier in Guangdong—under Zhao's direction. These policies bear his mark. We have witnessed elements of these policies in his work and writings throughout the 1950s, and we will see that they become his trademark throughout the remainder of his career. To be sure, other leaders at the center shared these policy preferences, but Zhao was often the one who implemented them locally and made them a successful model for emulation which conservative national leaders could seize on.

During the spring and fall of 1960 Zhao maintained a high public profile. In January he gave "important instructions" to the First Guangdong Agricultural Machinery Conference, and met with the visiting East German Deputy Prime Minister. From 29 February to 9 March he attended and delivered a report to a provincial conference of "Cadres of Six Levels." In early April he attended and gave "instructions" to a provincial conference of militia representatives. In September he attended a reception at the Vietnamese Consulate. In October he hosted visitors from Burma and Ceylon, and in late November he attended the Third Session of the Second Guangdong People's Congress.[101] His public disappearance during the summer remains unexplained.

To sum up Zhao's career from 1954 to 1960, we may conclude that the man essentially matured as a politician in the Chinese system. In a sense, he matured along with the system. He ascended many rungs on the career ladder, gained experience in a wide variety of issue-areas, and performed a wide range of duties. In other words, he was becoming a political generalist—a necessary credential for upward career mobility and national office in China.[102] He defined more clearly his own policy preferences and developed a functional area of expertise in agriculture. He began to articulate his policy preferences publicly, and on the whole did not abandon these policies when they were under attack. He also learned the rules of the game of political survival. When he sensed that his preferences were not in vogue, he disappeared from public view (often for months at a time), managed to avoid criticism, and resurfaced when the policy was modified. This was the case during parts of collectivization, the Anti-Rightist Campaign, and the Great Leap Forward. Lastly, he both cultivated and was cultivated by a patron (Tao Zhu) and met the key national leaders—unquestionably helpful attributes to career advancement in the Chinese political system. It is equally important to note, however, that though he had a patron, there is no real evidence that he had clients of his own. Li Jinjia and Li Ziyuan, who worked closely with Zhao on the Land Reform Committee and Rural Work Department, come the closest, but their relationships with Zhao appear to be more as colleagues than clients. By 1960 Zhao had risen quickly through the provincial apparatus, and while not yet having reached the pinnacle of provincial power (first Party secretary), he was well positioned to rise further.

NOTES

1. Nanfang Ribao (hereafter NFRB), 2 August 1954.

2. See A. Doak Barnett, Communist China: The Early Years, 1949-55 (New York, 1964), ch. 20.

3. NFRB, 2 October 1954.

4. Who's Who in Communist China (Hong Kong, 1970 revised ed.), Vol. I, p. 74.

5. NFRB, 7 February 1955; Wen Hui Bao (Hong Kong), 8 February 1955.

6. Who's Who in Communist China, Vol. I, p. 74; China Aktuell Supplement, PRC Biographical Activities (September 1980), p. 40.

7. Wen Hui Bao (Hong Kong), 23 August 1955.

8. Zhong Gong Ming Lu (Taipei, revised ed., 1978), pp. 87-88. It should be pointed out that this is the only source which identifies Zhao in this post at this time.

9. China Auktuell (September 1980), p. 40; Who's Who in Communist China, Vol. I, p. 74.

10. NFRB, 20 November 1957.

11. A. Doak Barnett, Cadres, Bureaucracy and Political Power in China (New York, 1967), pp. 202-3. The following section on specific duties relating to Zhao's official positions draws on Barnett, especially pp. 135-36, 139-42, and 147-53.

12. Zhong Gong Ming Lu, pp. 87-88.

13. Zhao's public appearances are reported in NFRB, 29 May 1955 and NFRB, 14 March 1956; New China News Agency (hereafter NCNA), 26 August 1955; NCNA, 28 January 1960; NFRB, 3 September 1960; NCNA, 11 October 1960; and NCNA, 12 October 1960, respectively.

14. For more on the GPD, see Glenn Dick, "The General Political Department," in William Whitson (Ed.), The Military and Political Power in China in the 1970s (New York, 1972), pp. 171-83.

15. See Kenneth Lieberthal, Central Documents and Politburo Politics in China (Ann Arbor, 1978); Michel Oksenberg, "Methods of Communication in the Chinese Bureaucracy," China Quarterly, No. 57 (January-March 1974), pp. 1-39.

16. See for example, Parris Chang, "Research Notes on the Changing Loci of Decision-Making in the CCP," China Quarterly, No. 44 (1970), pp. 181-94.

17. Barnett, Cadres, Bureaucracy, and Political Power, p. 136.

18. Ibid.

19. See Vivienne Shue, Peasant China in Transition (Berkeley, 1980), ch. 3.

20. NFRB, 25 November 1955.

21. As cited in Vogel (from official Chinese sources), Canton Under Communism (Cambridge, 2d ed., 1980), Appendix B, Table 8, p. 377.

22. Ibid., pp. 139, 377.

23. Ibid., p. 139.

24. Ibid.

26

25. NFRB, 9 June 1955, as cited in Vogel, Canton Under Communism, p. 140.

26. Roderick MacFarquhar, The Origins of the Cultural Revolution, Vol. I (New York, 1974), pp. 16-19.

27. NFRB, 9, 24 June 1955, as cited in Vogel, Canton Under Communism, p. 146.

28. Mao Zedong, "On the Cooperative Transformation of Agriculture," in Selected Works of Mao Zedong, Vol. V (Beijing, 1977), pp. 184-207.

29. See Michel Oksenberg, "The Chinese Policy Process and the Public Health Issue: An Arena Approach," in Studies in Comparative Communism, Vol. VII, No. 4 (Winter 1974), pp. 375-408.

30. NFRB, 21 September 1955.

31. Vogel, Canton Under Communism, p. 150.

32. NFRB, 8 September 1955, as cited in Vogel, ibid., p. 150.

33. NFRB, 8 November 1955.

34. NFRB, 8 November 1955.

35. NFRB, 11 February 1956, as cited in Vogel, Canton Under Communism, p. 155.

36. Kenneth Lieberthal, A Research Guide to Central Party and Government Meetings in China, 1949-75 (White Plains, 1976), pp. 75-76.

37. Ibid., pp. 78-79.

38. Ibid. Deng Zihui was absent from this meeting.

39. A good analysis of this document can be found in Parris Chang, Power and Policy in China (University Park, 2d ed., 1978), pp. 17-23.

40. NFRB, 8 April 1956, as cited in Chang, Power and Policy, p. 21.

41. NFRB, 25, 27 February 1956.

42. A good description of these can be found in Chang, Power and Policy, p. 29; Lieberthal, Central Meetings, pp. 83-84.

43. I wish to thank Dorothy Solinger for bringing this to my attention.

44. Zhao appeared at an agricultural exhibition in February (see NFRB, 25 February 1956), and at the Polish Consulate in March to express condolences for Boleslaw Bierut, first secretary of the Polish United Workers Party (see NCNA, Guangzhou, 14 March 1956).

45. NFRB, 26 August 1956.

46. NFRB, 23 February 1957.

47. NFRB, 4 May 1957, as cited by Vogel, Canton Under Communism, p. 190.

48. NFRB, 23 April 1957, as cited by Vogel, ibid., p. 191.

49. NCNA, Guangzhou, 2 May 1957.

50. See for example Vogel, Canton Under Communism, pp. 193-99; Roderick MacFarquhar, The Hundred Flowers Campaign and the Chinese Intellectuals (New York, 1960), pp. 233-35.

51. NCNA, Guangzhou, 14 May 1957.

52. There are a number of good analyses of the Hundred Flowers criticisms, particularly Frederick Teiwes, Politics and Purges in China: Rectification and the Decline of Party Norms, 1950-1965 (White Plains, 1979), ch. 6; MacFarquhar, Origins of the Cultural Revolution, chs. 15 and 16; MacFarquhar, The Hundred Flowers Campaign. Similarly, for discussion of the ensuing Anti-Rightist Campaign, see these same sources.

53. NFRB, 26 July 1957.

54. NFRB, 20 November 1957.

55. For a more extensive analysis of this campaign, see Teiwes, Politics and Purges, pp. 323-26.

56. Vogel, Canton Under Communism, p. 205.

57. Vogel, ibid.

58. NFRB, 7 December 1957.

59. NFRB, 8 December 1957, as cited in Vogel, Canton Under Communism, pp. 204-5, 207.

60. See Vogel, Canton Under Communism, pp. 118, 122, 211-16; Teiwes, Politics and Purges, p. 370; Frederick Teiwes, Provincial Party Personnel in Mainland China, 1956-66 (New York, 1967), pp. 17-18, 22.

61. The text is provided in URS, Vol. 13, No. 14, pp. 196-206.

62. Donald Klein and Ann Clark, Biographic Dictionary of Chinese Communism, Vol. 1 (Cambridge, 1971), pp. 281-82.

63. Ibid., p. 450.

64. Union Research Service (hereafter URS), Vol. 13, No. 14, pp. 196-206.

65. In retrospect, a contributing factor to Zhao's earlier absences may have been related to Feng's and Gu's senior status and resentment of Zhao as a "northerner."

66. Vogel, Canton Under Communism, p. 227.

67. NCNA, Guangzhou, 28 December 1957.

68. Vogel, Canton Under Communism, p. 237.

69. NFRB, 28 February 1958.

70. NFRB, 15 February 1958.

71. NFRB, 12, 29 May 1958.

72. NFRB, 4 May 1958.

73. NFRB, 23 April 1958; and NCNA, Guangzhou, 25 May 1958, respectively.

74. Renmin Ribao (hereafter RMRB), 30 May 1958; translated in Current Background (hereafter CB), No. 509, 10 June 1958, pp. 59-64.

75. Ibid.

76. Ibid., "The Present State of Guangdong Grain Production," Shangyu, No. 2, 1 September 1958; "Experiences in Managing Late Rice Production in Guangdong," RMRB, 18 November 1958; "On the New Stage in Agricultural Production," Zhongguo Qingnian Bao, No. 4, 23 February 1959; "Fight for 100 Billion Catties of Grain," Shangyu, No. 5, 10 March 1959; "Basic Methods in the Reform of Agricultural Technology," RMRB, 4 June 1959; "Great Achievements, Rich Experiences," NFRB, 1 October 1959; "We Must Realize an Especially Great Leap Forward in Hog Raising," NFRB, 5 February 1960; "Agriculture Must Be Specially Developed," NFRB, 17 March 1960; "Let the Whole Party Seize Agriculture," NFRB, 14 July 1960.

77. Tao Zhu, "Ways of Looking at Three Problems," Shangyu No. 3, 1 October 1958; Zhao Ziyang, "Guangdong's Experience in Leading the Raising of Late Crops," RMRB, 18 November 1958.

78. Da Gong Bao (Hong Kong), 6 December 1958.

79. Anne Thurston, Authority and Legitimacy in Post-Revolution Rural Guangdong: The Case of the People's Communes (Ph.D. dissertation, University of California-Berkeley, 1975), pp. 289-94.

80. Ibid., pp. 312-13.

81. SCMP, No. 1932, pp. 21-23. Also see Vogel, Canton Under Communism, p. 258.

82. RMRB, 25 February 1959.

83. NFRB, 1 March 1959; SCMP, No. 1996, pp. 38-42; Vogel, Canton Under Communism, p. 257.

84. "Sixteen Articles Concerning Work Methods," Miscellany of Mao Zedong Thought, Joint Publications Research Service (hereafter JPRS), Report No. 61269-1 (20 February 1964), p. 179. This source is a translation of Mao Zedong Sixiang Wansui!

85. See Roderick MacFarquhar, The Origins of the Cultural Revolution, Vol. II: The Great Leap Forward (New York, 1983), pp. 141-42. This book is a thorough account of the Great Leap Forward.

86. MacFarquhar, ibid., pp. 144, 156-59.

87. NCNA, Beijing, 19 March 1959.

88. Zhao Ziyang, "On Fundamental Ways for Reforming Agricultural Technology," RMRB, 4 June 1959.

89. RMRB, 3 June 1959; SCMP, No. 2032, 11 June 1959.

90. NFRB, 27 May 1959; SCMP, No. 2072, 27 May 1959.

91. Thurston, Authority and Legitimacy, pp. 318-19.

92. Vogel, Canton Under Communism, p. 254.

93. RMRB, 18 June 1959, as cited in Peter R. Moody, Jr., "Policy and Power: The Career of Tao Zhu, 1956-66," in China Quarterly, No. 54 (1973).

94. See Lieberthal, Central Meetings, pp. 141-45.

95. See Union Research Institute, The Case of Peng Dehuai (Hong Kong, 1968); David Charles, "The Dismissal of Marshal Peng Dehuai," The China Quarterly, No. 8 (October-December 1961), pp. 63-76.

96. See Chinese Law and Government, Vol. I, No. 4 (Winter 1968-1969).

97. See Charles, "The Dismissal of Marshal Peng Dehuai."

98. See Teiwes, Politics and Purges, ch. 9.

99. NFRB, 8 October 1959.

100. It was not officially abandoned until after the Beidaihe work conference in July.

101. For reports on these appearances see, respectively: NFRB, 13 January 1960; NCNA, Guangzhou, 24 and 28 January 1960; NFRB, 17 March 1960; NFRB, 2 and 7 April 1960; NFRB, 3 September 1960; NCNA, Guangzhou, 11, 12, 13 October 1960; and Da Gong Bao (Hong Kong), 30 November 1960.

102. See Michel Oksenberg and Yeung Sai-cheung. "Hua Guo-feng's Pre-Cultural Revolution Hunan Years, 1949-66: The Making of a Political Generalist," China Quarterly, No. 69 (March 1977).

3
Capitalizing on the Economy and Campaigning for Power, 1961–1965

Economic recovery from the Great Leap fiasco dominated the leaders' agenda, both at the center and in the provinces, during the early 1960s. Conservative leaders and policies took command as never before in post-1949 China. To be sure, they were not unchallenged. As we will see, the Socialist Education Movement became the main vehicle for those who sought to undermine the conservative leaders and policies. At the center, the main conservative leaders were Liu Shaoqi, Deng Xiaoping, Chen Yun, Bo Yibo, Deng Zihui, Li Fuchun, Peng Zhen, Zhou Yang, and Lu Dingyi. They coordinated the drafting of a series of policy documents aimed at, among other things, restoring experts to a primary place in economic planning, increasing central bureaucratic control, and using material incentives as an engine to drive economic growth.[1] These policy documents were dubbed the "Sixty Articles on Agriculture," "Seventy Articles on Industry," "Fourteen Articles on Science," "Six Articles on Finance," "Sixty Articles on Education," "Eight Articles on Literature and Art," "Thirty-five Articles on Handicraft Trades," and a "Decision on Commercial Work." These documents contained a number of quasi-capitalist programs, many of which would be used as evidence of "revisionism" and "taking the capitalist road" when these conservative leaders were attacked during the Cultural Revolution.

With these individuals and policies gaining currency at the center, Tao Zhu and Zhao consolidated their power in Guangdong. For his part, Zhao continued to rise in rank during this period. In December 1961 he was promoted to second secretary of the Guangdong Party apparatus while remaining as secretary-general of the Secretariat. In January 1964 he was identified as political commissar of the Guangdong Military District. In June 1964 he was identified as secretary of the Secretariat of the Central-South Bureau (which was revived in early 1961). Also in 1964, Zhao was identified in three other comparatively undistinguished positions: member of the Guangdong Congress of Advanced Units, Producers and Workers in

Agriculture; member of the Presidium of the Guangdong Conference of "Five Good" Representatives in Industry and Communications Systems; and member of the Presidium of the Guangdong Congress of Advanced Young Intellectuals Going or Returning to the Countryside. Then in April 1965, after Tao Zhu had been appointed a vice premier (at the January NPC), Zhao succeeded Tao as first secretary of the Guangdong CCP. This was no small achievement; he had risen to the pinnacle of provincial power. At the age of forty-six, Zhao was the youngest first secretary in the nation.

As Zhao's positions multiplied and increased in importance, so did his public visibility. He gave several public speeches and work reports at conferences, made a number of publicized inspection tours throughout the province, continued to publish articles in the local and central press, and met with numerous foreigners passing through Guangzhou.

Zhao remained relatively inactive publicly during 1961 (appearing only in February, July, and October).[2] The first indication of his increased stature came in December 1961 at the Second Guangdong CCP Congress, when Zhao was assigned to give the main work report on "the current situation and tasks." In his report, Zhao endorsed the new ordering of economic priorities emanating from the center in the form of the "Sixty Articles on Agriculture" and the "Seventy Articles on Industry." These policies (which went by the rubric of "readjustment, consolidation, filling out and raising standards" (tiaozheng gonggu chongshi tigao) placed first priority on agriculture and light industrial production, to meet consumer needs. In agriculture, the production team was made the basic accounting unit and the policies of sanzi yibao and dangan hu were reactivated. In industry, capital construction programs were terminated, investment was diverted from heavy to light industry, and the piece-rate wage system was restored. Zhao's report enthusiastically reflected these policy changes:

> The crux of the effort at securing a turn for the better in the economic situation is to secure a turn for the better in agriculture, first of all to gain a big bumper harvest by next year in order to be able to further improve the livelihood of the peasants, and to supply the cities and industry with more grains, subsidiary foodstuffs and light industrial raw materials. The principle guarantee for a big increase in farm production next year is to be sought in the implementation of the policy of unifying the right of production and that of distribution in the hands of the production teams so as to further consolidate the three-level system of ownership of the people's communes. . . . To help agriculture get a better harvest next year, industry must go all out to produce means of agricultural production and light industrial articles of everyday use of handicraft products to meet the needs of agriculture.[3]

Since Zhao was an "agriculture-first" man, the new policies were clearly to his liking.

In early 1962 Tao and Zhao hosted two national conferences in Guangzhou. The National Conference on Scientific and Technological Work was convened from 14-28 February and adopted the "Fourteen Articles on Science." The National Conference for the Creation of Dramas and Operas was convened from 3-26 March and adopted the "Eight Articles on Literature and Art." Both conferences sought to restore expertise and more freedom of expression in their respective fields.[4] Undoubtedly Guangzhou was chosen as the site for these meetings not only for the purpose of escaping the Beijing winter, but also because Tao and Zhao were implementing policies to the liking of conservative central leaders.

The conservative leaders and their policies were dominant throughout a series of meetings in the spring and early summer.[5] However, with the central work conference held at Beidaihe from late July to 19 September, and the ensuing Tenth Plenum, a counterattack was launched by Chairman Mao. At Beidaihe the Chairman launched his comeback from "the second line" in a forceful way by:

— stressing the need for continued "class struggle";

— warning of the possibility of capitalist and feudal restoration;

— calling for a campaign of "socialist education";

— criticizing Chen Yun and Li Xiannian by name for undermining the collective economy and facilitating private farming;

— ousting Deng Zihui as Director of the Rural Work Department and the State Council's Agricultural and Forestry Staff Office;

— complaining that the State Planning Commission (headed by Li Fuchun), the State Economic Commission (headed by Bo Yibo), and the Finance and Trade Staff Office of the State Council (headed by Li Xiannian) had become "independent kingdoms"; and

— criticizing Liu Shaoqi for having pursued a "rightist" policy line.[6]

The Chairman had reasserted himself. He continued to voice his concerns at the Tenth Plenum, which he presided over, and made his famous call to "never forget class struggle." The plenum essentially adopted the conclusions of the work conference as the official Party line. Three documents were approved: (1) the Resolution on Strengthening Collective Economy, (2) the Revised Sixty Articles on Agriculture, and (3) the Decision on Commercial Work. Despite Mao's input to the drafting of all three documents, the final content was not to his liking. The Resolution centered on the "technical reform" of agriculture, the Decision adopted Chen Yun and Li

Xiannian's proposal for the "unified supply" of commodities, and the Revised Sixty Articles retained the <u>sanzi yibao</u> as its centerpiece.[7]

In the months following the plenum, Tao Zhu and others in the Guangdong hierarchy paid only lip service to Mao's call for class struggle, but did nothing practical to foster it, such as to convene meetings or organize work teams.[8] Zhao, for instance, only made a statement that literature and drama should reflect class struggle.[9] The Guangdong People's Council, which met on 18-19 October supposedly to implement the Tenth Plenum's directives, did not even mention "class struggle" but rather stressed the "technical reform" of agriculture.[10] Although the phrase "politics in command" was used in the communique, it was to be in command "in order to serve production."[11] Zhao's influence was evident. While Tao and Zhao ignored Mao's call for class struggle in most realms, they did respond to his plea for a renewed <u>xiafang</u> (downward transfer) policy for cadres. This policy directed that cadres at all levels were to "go down" to the countryside in work teams and "penetrate a point" (<u>shenru dao yige dian</u>) by "squatting at a point" (<u>dundian</u>). In essence, what this meant was that these work teams were to enter production brigades and teams, live among the "masses," investigate (<u>diaocha</u>) their conditions, and help to organize their work. Between November 1962 and February 1963 in Guangdong, it was reported that 30,000 cadres from the provincial, special district, county, and commune levels entered basic-level units and "squatted."[12] Aside from overseeing this movement, there is no direct evidence that Zhao personally "squatted," although he was absent from public view from December 1961 to April 1962, from early May to early August, and from mid-October to January 1963.[13] Given that throughout his career Zhao had demonstrated a penchant for on-site investigation, it is not unreasonable to expect that he too may have "gone down" to the countryside to "squat."

This movement demonstrates the earliest phase of the Socialist Education Movement (SEM). The SEM was the main vehicle through which the Chairman and his allies contested the aforementioned reforms in rural policy and, in many ways, was the harbinger to the Cultural Revolution. The SEM was discussed at a Central Committee meeting in February and officially launched at a central work conference in May 1963. The conference adopted the "Draft Resolution on Some Problems in Current Rural Work" (known as the "First Ten Points"). This document, which clearly reflected Mao's preferences, was a sweeping indictment of the conservatives' rural policy.[14] Among other things, it launched the "Four Clean-ups" campaign (<u>siqing</u>). This campaign was aimed at cleaning up cadre corruption in accounting, granary inventories, properties, and work points. In Guangdong, Zhao was put in charge of administering the campaign by being appointed the director of the provincial "Four Clean-ups" Office Leading Small Group. He directed that the special districts and <u>xian</u> Party committees establish "work corps" (gongzuo duan) and the communes establish work teams. He further organized work teams (gongzuo dui) from the provincial Four Clean-ups Office, comprised of Party cadres, government cadres, and PLA soldiers, which were to proceed to selected teams and brigades during the summer of 1963.[15] Did Zhao direct his work teams to "squat," organize poor and lower-middle peasant associations, and inculcate the peasantry with socialist values as the central directives had stipulated? Yes, but, true to form, Zhao stressed that the campaign was aimed at increasing production and construction. Its real aim, Zhao said, was to "build the poor countryside into an affluent, socialist, new countryside."[16] Thus, we again find Zhao manipulating and distorting central directives for the sake of maintaining production. By August Zhao was confident enough about the way that the SEM was unfolding in the province that he gave an upbeat assessment of the campaign's effect on the upcoming fall harvest in a summary report to a provincial economic work conference.[17] In his report, Zhao also dwelled on the importance of the free market (ziyou shichang) in insuring a good distribution of the harvest.[18]

Because he did not want this campaign to disrupt production, Zhao welcomed the promulgation of the central directive "Some Concrete Policy Formulations in the Rural Socialist Education Movement" (the Second or Later Ten Points) in September. This directive, drafted by Deng Xiaoping and Peng Zhen,[19] substantially modified the spirit and softened the impact of the SEM, as embodied in the First Ten Points. The new directive, among other things, demanded that "at no stage of the movement should production be affected" and that "measures taken during the course of the movement should be helpful to production."[20] The directive further reaffirmed the validity of the sanzi yibao policy and stated that the 1962 Revised Sixty Articles on Agriculture should be a measure in judging the proper implementation of the SEM. Zhao repeated these themes, while not even mentioning class struggle, in his speech to a provincial agricultural work conference held from 21-29 December 1963.[21]

During the first six months of 1964, the conservatives' reinterpretation of the SEM, as embodied in the Second Ten Points, continued to prevail at the center and in Guangdong. In February Tao Zhu published an article on communes in the People's Daily in which he stressed: "We are still in the stage of socialism, and current ownership and distribution policies should continue. He who does not work, neither shall he eat. Use material incentives. Oppose egalitarianism. Raise the peasants' standard of living."[22] Also in early 1964, when addressing "advanced representatives" of the PLA Guangdong Military District on the proper implementation of the national "Learn from the PLA" campaign, Tao and Zhao (in his capacity as political commissar) stressed the importance of maintaining a "high tide" in production.[23] This is not what the Chairman had in mind in launching the emulation campaign. It was another attempt by Mao to regain control of the SEM, this time by using his favorite tactic of going outside the Party apparatus and using another organization—this time the PLA—to take his case to the masses and control the Party. This was the beginning of the PLA's active intervention into the political arena (and Lin Biao's concomitant rise) which would grow steadily during the next seven years, culminating in the reconstituted post-Cultural Revolution Revolutionary Committees.

Perhaps in response to the Chairman's new initiative—or in the hope of currying favor with the Chairman—Zhao published an article titled "The Great Significance of the Revolutionization of the Thought of Man" in the People's Daily on 4 April. This article expressed Zhao's interpretation of Mao's 1957 article "On the Correct Handling of Contradictions Among the People." In his article, Zhao repeatedly praised the Chairman's "brilliant thought" and quoted him several times. This is indeed patronizing and somewhat out of character for Zhao, but it must be remembered that this was a necessary rule of the political game during Mao's tenure; it was also a tactic frequently used by provincial secretaries who felt under pressure and wanted to prove their loyalty to the Chairman.[24] But why did Zhao decide to review Mao's seven-year-old article at this particular time? One reason is because it enabled him to address the issue of class struggle (which he had previously avoided) and discuss it as a "non-antagonistic contradiction" existing "among the people," which should henceforth be handled peacefully so as not to disrupt production. Unity, not divisiveness, was his theme. Only through "the people's unity" could production be maintained. This is the upshot of Zhao's article. These themes are evident in the following salient passages:

> In the past year or so, we have launched a socialist education movement in accordance with the instructions of Comrade Mao Zedong in all rural and urban areas of the province. The large number of facts revealed during the movement once more vividly and effectively proves that classes, class contradictions, and class struggle still exist in a socialist society. . . . Therefore, our socialist construction is always intricately interwoven with the socialist revolution. While carrying out socialist construction, it is necessary to carry out socialist revolution in a coordinated manner, and while engaged in production struggle and scientific experiment, we must also carry out class struggle appropriately. . . . The formula of "unity-criticism-unity" summed up for us by Comrade Mao Zedong generalizes this idea most profoundly. . . . In dealing with contradictions among the people, it is essential to start with the desire for unity, without which it will be impossible to realize the objective of

rallying more than 95 percent of the cadres and the popular masses. In handling contradictions among the people, it is also necessary to adopt the correct method, that is, the method of persuasive education. Failure to adopt this method will not allow people to carry out self-revolution consciously.[25]

Thus we again see Zhao distorting the intent of a radical national campaign, while airing his views in a national forum and trying to gain support from national elites.

One national elite whose support Zhao sought was Liu Shaoqi. During the summer of 1964, Liu and his wife Wang Guangmei toured the provinces (sometimes incognito). In July they visited Guangdong and Zhao was their escort. Upon the completion of their visit, Zhao was quoted as saying: "Comrade Liu Shaoqi's instructions and Comrade Wang Guangmei's report on the 'Taoyuan Experience' are extremely important in carrying out well the Socialist Education Movement in urban and rural areas. . . . With Comrade Liu's instructions and Comrade Wang's report, we have found a good method."[26] Upon his return to Beijing in September, and the promulgation of the Revised Draft of the Second Ten Points,[27] Liu had managed to wrest control of the SEM from Mao, who had seized the initiative in June at a central work conference by listing six criteria for measuring the success of the campaign.[28] These criteria made the cadre rectification issue an "antagonistic contradiction," but after Liu's resurgence the People's Daily National Day editorial asserted (like Zhao's April article) that: "The great historical significance of the Socialist Education Movement lies in the following fact—it is a movement for educating the cadres and masses in the revolutionary spirit of the general line and for correctly handling contradictions among the people" (emphasis added).[29]

In Maoist lexicon "contradictions among the people" are "nonantagonistic contradictions," which means that they are to be settled through peaceful criticism where an individual can repent by admitting one's misguided ways and will be permitted to continue on in one's job. If the person is a Party cadre the criticism will take place only inside the Party, so-called "closed door rectification" (guanmen zhengfeng). On the other hand, if the contradiction is an "antagonistic" one between "the enemy and the people," criticism and punishment know no bounds. The person is to be "struggled against" without limits, and death may result as punishment. If the person is a cadre, the "masses" will do the criticizing and punishing, so-called "open door rectification" (kaimen zhengfeng). Throughout his career, Liu Shaoqi favored the former technique, while Mao frequently resorted to the latter. The fifth of Mao's aforementioned "six criteria" stipulated: "When landlords, rich peasants, counterrevolutionaries and bad elements who engage in destructive activities are discovered, is this contradiction merely turned over to the higher levels, or are the masses mobilized to strictly supervise, criticize and even appropriately struggle against these elements, and moreover retain them for reform on the spot?"[30] Thus, during the fall of 1964, Liu was not following Mao's criteria at all. He was attacking cadre corruption, not revisionism, and was using large work teams, rather than the masses, to undertake investigation and criticism.

Where was Zhao during this period? After having remained publicly active at ceremonial functions during the latter half of the summer, he curiously dropped from public view from late May to late July and again during the fall.[31] He made only one reported public appearance after the mid-September provincial People's Congress. One can only speculate that he knew that there were conflicting policy tendencies at the center and he decided to wait until they became clarified. The one available indication of his whereabouts, which might explain his early summer disapperance, comes from none other than Mao Zedong. At an "anti-revisionism" meeting on 4 September 1964, Mao is reported as saying, "Why then did Zhao Ziyang live in a poor old peasants home to feed dogs? He was afraid others might get him."[32]

The conflict at the center only became more intense. In January 1965 Mao counterattacked again. In its New Year editorial the People's Daily shifted course 180 degrees from its National Day editorial by stating bluntly: "The principal contradiction in China today is the antagonistic contradiction between socialism and capitalism. . . . The Socialist Education Movement now unfolding in the urban and rural areas is directed precisely at carrying further the resolution of this contradiction."[33] Later in January, at a central work conference of the Politburo, Mao was able to promulgate a new directive which again shifted the emphasis of the SEM. This directive, "Some Problems Currently Arising in the Course of the Rural Socialist Education Movement," was dubbed the "Twenty-Three Articles." It stressed that "antagonistic class contradictions" were to be the main focus of the SEM in the future. But no longer was the campaign to be directed only at low-level cadres. As the Twenty-Three Articles put it:

> The key point of this Movement is to rectify those people of author-
> ity within the Party who take the capitalist road . . . of these people
> . . . some are out in the open and some remain concealed. Of the
> people who support them, some are at lower levels and some at
> higher levels, there are some people in the communes, districts,
> counties, special districts, and even in the work of Provincial and
> Central Committee departments, who oppose socialism (emphasis
> added).[34]

The directive further stated explicitly that leading personnel from the regional bureaus of the Central Committee must "squat at points" in the countryside.

Tao Zhu reportedly "squatted" from September 1964 through June 1965 (under the alias "Section Chief Jin") in Xinhe brigade of Huashan commune, Hua xian.[35] While there, Tao reportedly exhorted the peasants to increase production. He is quoted as having said, "Whether or not the Four Clean-ups are a success depends on the increase or decrease in output.[36] During the month of March Zhao also "squatted" at the Guzhong brigade of Huanzheng commune in Zhongshan xian. While there, he was not struggled against but, on the contrary, spent much time giving instructions to various groups in the county. He spoke to rusticated youths about the merits of living in the countryside;[37] he visited the county medical college and gave a talk on rural public health work;[38] and he attended a week-long conference of cadres from "three levels" in Xinhui (the county seat) where he gave another talk exhorting them to push forward the "compare, learn, overtake, help" campaign in order to "accelerate production at high speed."[39] Many of Zhao's activities were reported on the front page of Nanfang Ribao.

The publicity helped Zhao's image, which had been tarnished one year earlier when Zhao had been very embarrassed by the "Shengshi Incident" in Zhongshan xian. The Shengshi brigade of Shaji commune was Guangdong's equivalent of Dazhai. While it did not have the extent of national publicity that Dazhai did, it was a provincial model and the Guangdong CCP Committee had called on all to "learn from Shengshi." Zhao was even on record in a national forum (People's Daily) for praising the brigade as an "advanced unit" and a model of "revolutionization."[40] Then, however, the brigade's secretary, Chen Hua, who had participated in meetings of SEM activists in Beijing, had met Chairman Mao, and was known nationally as something of a southern counterpart to Dazhai's Chen Yonggui, was accused by a poor peasant of embezzling the brigade's public funds for his private use and raping a peasant's wife.[41] After two work teams dispatched by Zhao's Four Clean-Ups Office failed to resolve the case, the peasants in the brigade who had charged Chen appealed directly to the General Office of the CCP Central Committee (zhongyang banggongshi). Soon a work team from the center arrived, headed by Wang Guangmei (in disguise) and a number of officials from the Public Security Bureau. When Chen realized the identity of this work team he realized that his days were numbered, and he attempted to flee to Hong Kong in a motorboat. He was caught, "struggled against," and jailed. He subsequently died, although by what means is debated. Some refugees report that he committed suicide in jail, but others claim that he either threw himself or was thrown onto a high-voltage transformer at the brigade headquarters.[42] This incident was potentially extremely embarrassing to Tao Zhu and Zhao who had previously lauded Chen Hua and the brigade. They were both forced to admit that the initial "squats" during the Four Clean-ups had been superficial, but on the whole they managed to cover up the "Shengshi Incident" and evade responsibility.

Another stipulation of the Twenty-Three Articles was that provincial Party committees should accelerate the pace of forming Poor and Lower Middle Peasant Associations (PLMPA). After returning to Guangzhou by 10 April, when he viewed the performance of "Surprise Attack on the White Tiger Regiment" put on by one of Jiang Qing's Beijing Opera troupes,[43] Zhao and the provincial Party committee convened a provincial PLMPA conference. Zhao delivered an "important speech" and was elected a member of the Association's standing committee.[44] Zhao remained publicly active throughout the summer of 1965 by meeting with various groups: recent Zhongshan University graduates, opera performers, rural mobile medical teams, and militiamen.[45]

Then in late August 1965 Zhao delivered an important speech entitled "First Place Must Be Given to Flexible Study and Application of Chairman Mao's Works in All Work" to a meeting in Guangzhou of "Activists to Exchange Experiences in Studying Chairman Mao's Works." This speech is indicative of the last phase of the SEM, which led into the Cultural Revolution. This phase of the SEM (to study Mao's works) was launched in the Central-South region and was aimed at rectification of Party cadres at the xian level.[46] They were to be subjected to intensive "criticism and self-criticism" in order to overcome "bureaucratism, conservatism, and commandism." "Political instructors" were sent into production brigades and teams to ensure that politics "took command" in the criticism. For example, with regard to the "contradiction between politics and production" many comrades were accused of holding the view that "good performances in production means good performance in politics." This was criticized on the ground that it failed to answer the question of whether production promoted the interests of the collective or the interests of private individuals.[47] By studying Mao's thought, cadres would theoretically be able to perceive the priority of collective interests.[48]

Did Zhao's speech stress these themes? In a word, yes. The speech of Zhao's is very out of character with his past policy dispositions. The following quotations will serve to illuminate this point. With regard to the direction of the movement Zhao said:

> Taking the picture of the province as a whole, however, the movement for studying Chairman Mao's works has not been developed universally and intensively, and the atmosphere of study has not been sufficiently strong. . . . The major problem is the failure of the

leadership to catch up with the situation. The leadership of the Party provincial committee, as well as the leadership of district, municipal, and xian Party committees, lags behind the situation and the masses. . . . The moment has now arrived for a thorough change in this state of affairs. The solution of this problem must begin with the provincial Party committee . . . the question of how to direct properly the movement for studying Chairman Mao's works in one's own area has not been put on the most important daily agenda of the Party committee.[49]

With regard to the important issue of the relationship between politics and production Zhao contradicts his past statements and behavior in a lengthy éxpose:

When politics is well, all will be well. When politics is advanced, construction, business, and technology will also be advanced. It is politics which commands production, business and technology. . . . Some people also hold: "Production is politics. Success in production is success in politics. When production is good, politics will naturally be good. Failure in production means failure in politics. Production is supreme and all other things are not. Production is above everything else." These ideas are a variety under new conditions of the purely military viewpoint which was criticized by Chairman Mao at the Gudian Conference a long time ago. In the same way as Chairman Mao criticized the purely military viewpoint at that conference, we must resolutely criticize this purely production, purely professional and purely technical viewpoint. We must hold a big debate within our Party and iron out the matter as to how we should correctly view the relationships between production and politics, between politics and business, and between politics and technique. If we occupy ourselves with production alone, does it mean that our production is good? Is it true that production is supreme and above everything else? Should first place be given to politics or production? How, then, should we answer these questions? We say: Only when politics is good will production be good. . . . In our socialist society, production is good because politics is good. Our good production is true, solid and lasting because it is building on the political consciousness of the broad masses of the people. It is the natural result of a true understanding of the meaning of labor on the part of the people . . . even if some achievements are obtained at one moment by means of the so-called material incentives or by means of commandism, they are not real but sham achievements . . . if we, for example, engage in production with capitalist methods, then, even if we gain some momentary results, we shall eventually embark on the wrong path. That is extremely dangerous" (emphasis added).[50]

With regard to the methods to be used in this phase of the movement, Zhao had this to say:

> When we speak of rectification now, we mean the study of the thought of Mao Zedong by the method of criticism and self-criticism. In study, the amount of things to be studied should be reduced while the number of study sessions should be increased. . . . Party committees at various levels, up to and including the provincial Party committee, should speedily further perfect and restore their own central study groups. Those groups which exist in form and hold sessions irregularly must be adjusted. . . . The leadership of study in the course of the socialist education movement must persist in the policy of flexible study and application of Chairman Mao's works" (emphasis added).[51]

In this speech we see a very different Zhao Ziyang than the one who has sided with Liu Shaoqi during earlier phases of the SEM, who has done his best during this and other campaigns to maintain production by minimizing the campaign's impact at the local level, who has consistently placed production over politics throughout his career, and who has repeatedly employed "capitalist methods" such as material incentives which he denounces in this speech. The obvious question is why the switch? Moreover, one wonders why Zhao even made the speech? We can only speculate on the answers to these questions because hard evidence is lacking, but they nevertheless deserve to be addressed. The following possible explanations exist. First, one must consider that Zhao believed what he said, that he had changed to become an ardent worshipper of the Chairman, that he had seen the wrongs of his past and that this is something of a self-criticism. This is very doubtful; individuals do not change so quickly or easily. A variant of this possibility is that he had temporarily changed, that he was just caught up in the enthusiasm of the time and/or was opportunistically changing with the shift in emphasis of the campaign. While this is not uncommon in Chinese politics, and Zhao had demonstrated such opportunism before, this reasoning is also not the whole story. Consider the timing of the speech. Zhao was not jumping on an already rolling bandwagon; he was in at the ground stage of the new phase (to study Mao's works) of the campaign. As previously mentioned, this phase was kicked off in the Central-South Region. One suspects that, given the increasing role of the PLA in the SEM, the new phase was launched at Lin Biao's behest. Lin was the Chairman's most zealous fan. Lin had commanded the Central-South Region in the early 1950s and had career ties to Tao Zhu dating from the Whampoa Military Academy. Therefore, I suggest that Lin and Tao might have put Zhao up to it. If this was the case, the speech was probably ghost-written for Zhao. This might explain the uncharacteristic language (for Zhao), including the following statement: "With a clearcut aim of study and a correct attitude toward study, the questions of methods of study will be solved more easily. The best method of study is the one described by Marshal Lin Biao" (emphasis added).[52] This latter line of argument seems most plausible, but there is no hard evidence to sustain it.

Less than two weeks after the publication of this speech, the "old Zhao" reemerged when he published an article in the People's Daily entitled "Make Use of the Method of 'One Dividing into Two' to Bring About a New High Tide in Agricultural Production." While still more ideological in tone than his previous writings, in this article Zhao returned to his favorite subject—increasing agricultural production:

At present, an important task before the leaders at all levels in our province is how to maintain the sustained development of the high tide in agricultural production under the present most favorable situation. We are of the opinion that it is necessary to persist in employing the dialectical method of "one dividing into two" . . . The object of using the method of "one dividing into two" to expose contradictions is to heighten our awareness and promote the transformation of contradictions, so that the advanced may become even more advanced, the backward may overtake the advanced and the latecomer can occupy a higher place, thus continually impelling the development of production. . . . However, we must also make use of the method of "one dividing into two" to analyze another aspect of practical work. This is the need to integrate the revolutionary effort with the spirit of seeking truth from facts to integrate the revolutionary enthusiasm with the scientific attitude, and to translate the effort into measures and action. . . . In this way, the high production enthusiasm and the revolutionary effort of the masses will engender an enormous material force, and the high tide of production will be more healthy and solidly roll forward. . . . In regard to work method and work style, we must lay emphasis on ideological work, on development of democracy—especially democracy of production—and guard against coercion and commandism. Technical reforms must be popularized according to local conditions, and everything must be tested. . . . In regard to production targets and production measures, we should unfold democratic discussion, and cannot act arbitrarily. Apart from this, we must energetically develop the role of the commune system ownership at three levels. We must also persist in taking the production team as the foundation, and developing the economy of the commune and the brigade through strengthening them, but not at the expense of the economy of the production team. At present, it is of primary importance to develop energetically the collective economy at the production team level. At the same time, attention must also be paid to making proper arrangements for commune members in domestic sideline production (emphases added).[53]

Not only does Zhao stress production (to the implicit exclusion of politics), but here we also see him advocating measures which two weeks earlier he was denouncing as "sham achievements" and "capitalist tendencies." This is further evidence that, for whatever reason, the previous speech was an abberation.

The year 1965 had been a very busy one for Zhao, and by the end of the year he was receiving increased exposure in the national media.[54] By this time Zhao had succeeded Tao Zhu (who was promoted to Beijing) as first Party secretary of Guangdong and, in so doing, became the youngest first secretary in the nation. Along with this elevated position and increased exposure Zhao had also become more politically vulnerable, as we will see in the next chapter.

NOTES

1. I am indebted to Kenneth Lieberthal for his analysis of this period.

2. In February he attended a banquet commemorating the eleventh anniversary of the Sino-Soviet Treaty of Friendship, Alliance, and Mutual Assistance (Nanfang Ribao, hereafter NFRB, 15 February 1961). In July he delivered a report at a rally to celebrate the fortieth anniversary of the CCP (New China News Agency, hereafter NCNA, Beijing, 1 July 1961), and on 1 October he attended the National Day celebrations in Guangzhou (NCNA, Guangzhou, 1 October 1961). As with Zhao's past disappearances, there exists no firm evidence to explain these prolonged public absences.

3. Zhao Ziyang, "Report on Current Situation and Tasks in Guangdong at Second Provincial Party Congress," NFRB, 17 December 1961, translated in Survey Mainland China Press (hereafter SCMP), No. 2821, 19 September 1962, pp. 12-17.

4. See Kenneth Lieberthal, A Research Guide to Central Party and Government Meetings in China (White Plains, 1976), pp. 181-85.

5. Ibid., pp. 185-88.

6. Ibid., p. 189; Parris Chang, Power and Policy in China (University Park, 2d ed., 1978), p. 142.

7. Byung-joon Ahn, Chinese Politics and the Cultural Revolution (Seattle, 1976), pp. 79-80.

8. Ezra Vogel, Canton Under Communism (Cambridge, 2d ed., 1980), p. 301.

9. NFRB, 10 November 1962, as cited in Vogel, ibid.

10. NFRB, 21 October 1962, as cited in Vogel, ibid., p. 302.

11. Ibid.

12. Renmin Ribao (hereafter RMRB), 23 February 1963, as reported in Richard Baum and Frederick Teiwes, Ssu-Ch'ing: The Socialist Education Movement of 1962-66 (Berkeley, 1968), p. 14.

13. In April Zhao was a member of the funeral committee for General Jiang Feng, deputy director of the Guangdong PLA General Political Department (NFRB, 9 April 1962). He appeared at a May Day rally and reception (NCNA, Guangzhou, 1 May 1962 and NFRB, 1 May 1962 and NFRB, 1 May 1962). In early August he was identified as having made an inspection tour of flooded areas in Guangdong (Shi Shi Shouce—Current Events Handbook, No. 15, 6 August 1962). In September he met visiting Vietnamese officials (NCNA, Guangzhou, 28 September 1962), and was a member of He Cheng's funeral committee (Yangcheng Wanbao, hereafter YCWB, 11 September 1962). He had been secretary-general of the Central-South Bureau's Propaganda Department. In October he attended National Day activities (NFRB, 1 October 1962), and met more visiting Vietnamese dignitaries (NCNA, Guangzhou, 16 and 17 October 1962).

Zhao's public appearances picked up markedly during 1963. He appeared every month except November. In January Zhao attended a New Year's reception (NFRB, 1 January 1963), and met with visiting representatives of the Japanese Communist Party (NCNA, Guangzhou, 10 January 1963) and the Indonesian Communist Party (NCNA, Guangzhou, 22 January 1963). In February Zhao appeared at a Spring Festival party for Guangzhou workers' representatives (NCNA, Guangzhou, 5 February 1963). In March Zhao and Ou Mengjue attended an art troupe's performance (NFRB, 7 March 1963). In April Zhao and Tao Zhu met with representatives of the Guangdong Heroes' Conference (NFRB, 5 April 1963). In May he attended a May Day rally (NCNA, Guangzhou, 1 May 1963) and met with visiting Albanians (NCNA, Guangzhou, 13 May 1963). In June Zhao attended the opening session of the Second Guangdong Militia Representatives' Conference (YCWB, 10 June 1963, and NFRB, 11 June 1963). On 31 July he attended an Army Day reception (YCWB, 1 August 1963). In August Zhao gave the summary report to a provincial economic work conference, in which he stressed the "question of markets" (NFRB, 8 August 1963), and attended the opening session of the Fourth Guangdong Communist Youth League Congress (YCWB, 20 August 1963). He is also reported as having addressed this meeting (Zhongguo Qingnian Bao, 12 September 1963). In September Zhao attended a reception of the Vietnamese Consulate (NCNA, Guangzhou, 2 September 1963). In October Zhao convened and addressed a forum on rice strain breeding (YCWB, 13 October 1963). In December he attended the First Session of the Third Guangdong People's Congress (NFRB, 18 December 1963), and was named a representative to the congress from Foshan municipality (NFRB, 22 December 1963).

14. The text and a good description of the content of the First Ten Points can be found in Baum and Teiwes, ibid.; see also Ahn, Chinese Politics and the Cultural Revolution, pp. 93-95; Chang, Power and Policy, pp. 147-50.

15. Ahn, Chinese Politics and the Cultural Revolution, pp. 99-100.

16. Frederick Teiwes, Politics and Purges in China: Rectification and the Decline of Party Norms, 1950-1965 (White Plains, 1979), p. 571; Ahn, ibid., p. 102; Vogel, Canton Under Communism, p. 315.

17. NFRB, 8 August 1963.

18. Teiwes, Politics and Power, pp. 533-34.

19. Ibid.

20. As cited in Chang, Power and Policy, p. 151; text in Baum and Teiwes, Ssu-Ch'ing, pp. 72-94.

21. NFRB, 9, 19, and 21 January 1964.

22. Tao Zhu, "The People's Communes are Making Progress," RMRB, 28 February 1964, as cited by Peter R. Moody, Jr., "Power and Policy: The Career of Tao Zhu, 1956-66," in China Quarterly, No. 54 (1973).

23. NFRB, 26 January 1964, as cited in Vogel, Canton Under Communism, p. 370; YCWB, 29 January 1964.

24. This is one frequently employed tactic noted by Parris Chang in "Provincial Party Leaders' Strategies for Survival During the Cultural Revolution," in Robert Scalapino (Ed.), Elites in the People's Republic of China (Seattle, 1972).

25. RMRB, 4 April 1964; translated in SCMP, No. 4085, December 1967, pp. 18-19.

26. Red Guard source cited in SCMP, No. 4085, December 1967, pp. 18-19.

27. Text in Baum and Teiwes, Ssu-Ch'ing (Appendix E).

28. See Chang, Power and Policy, p. 152.

29. RMRB, 1 October 1964, as cited in Baum and Teiwes, Ssu-Ch'ing, p. 34.

30. As cited in Chang, Power and Policy, p. 152.

31. During 1954 Zhao appeared every month except March, June, November, and December. In January he attended a New Year's reception (NFRB, 1 January 1964), attended and addressed the Guangdong Advanced Agricultural Producers' and Workers' Conference (NFRB, 9 and 21 January 1964), and made an "important report" to a conference of representatives from the "four-good" units and "five-good" fighters of the Guangdong Military District (YCWB, 29 January 1964). In February he hosted a

Japanese Communist Party delegation (NCNA, Guangzhou, 15 and 16 February 1964). In April he was a member of the funeral committee for Ma Shiceng, director of the Guangdong Opera Theater (NFRB, 23 April 1964). In May Zhao was listed as a member of the Presidium for the Guangdong Representative Conference of "Four-Good" Units and "Five-Good" Workers in Industry, Commerce, Handicraft Industry, and Civil Transportation (NFRB, 24 May 1964). In July Zhao addressed the Second Guangdong CCP Congress (NFRB, 26 July 1964) and attended a reception for "Representatives of the Third Guangdong Conference of Activists in Socialist Construction Among Dependents of Martyrs and Servicemen, Disabled, Demobilized and Retired Servicemen, Veteran Revolutionaries, and Advanced Units in Relief Work (NFRB, 26 July 1964). In August Zhao attended a meeting of down-to-the countryside (xiaxiang) youth (Zhongguo Qingnian Bao, 25 August 1964). In September Zhao attended the Second Session of the Third Guangdong People's Congress (Wen Hui Bao, Hong Kong, 13 September 1964), and was a member of the funeral committee of Wang Weiguang, who was vice-chairman of the Planning Commission of the Central South Bureau (NFRB, 17 September 1964). In October Zhao was a member of the funeral committee for An Tianzong, who was vice-chairman of the Guangdong Economic Planning Commission (NFRB, 25 October 1964).

32. "Interjections at an Anti-Revisionist Report Meeting," Miscellany of Mao Zedong Thought, Joint Publications Reseach Service (hereafter JPRS), Report No. 61269-1 (20 February 1974), p. 421.

33. RMRB, 1 January 1965, as cited in Baum and Teiwes, Ssu-Ch'ing, p. 35.

34. Ibid., p. 37.

35. "Tao Zhu Is the Khrushchev of Central-South China," Current Background (hereafter CB), No. 824, 17 April 1967, pp. 10-17.

36. Ibid., p. 12.

37. NFRB, 18 March 1965.

38. NFRB, 14 March 1965.

39. NFRB, 22 March 1965.

40. RMRB, 4 April 1964; SCMP, No. 3220, 15 May 1964, pp. 4-5, 8-9.

41. This story is described in Ahn, Chinese Politics and the Cultural Revolution, pp. 101-2; and Richard Baum, Prelude to Revolution: Mao, the Party, and the Peasant Question, 1962-66 (New York, 1975), pp. 112-17.

42. Ibid., p. 102.

43. NFRB, 11 April 1965.

44. YCWB, 28 June 1965.

45. These appearances are reported in: YCWB, 12 June 1965; YCWB, 28 June 1965; YCWB, 21 June 1965; and YCWB, 1 August 1965, respectively.

46. Baum and Teiwes, Ssu-Ch'ing, p. 48.
47. Ibid., p. 43.
48. Ibid.
49. YCWB, 8 September 1965; translation in SCMP, No. 3540, 20 September 1965, p. 2.
50. Ibid., pp. 4-6.
51. Ibid., pp. 8, 10, 12.
52. Ibid., p. 7.
53. RMRB, 10 September 1965; translated in SCMP, No. 3552, pp. 10-18.
54. During 1965 Zhao appeared publicly every month except May and November. In January Zhao attended a Spring Festival celebration (NFRB, 1 February 1965). In February Zhao attended a sports exhibition (RMRB, 3 February 1965), and a meeting to encourage Guangzhou municipality peasants to attain a bumper harvest (NFRB, 10 February 1965). On 9 February Zhao, Tao Zhu, Ou Mengjue and others led a march to condemn "U.S. Imperialism's War Crimes in Vietnam," and their photograph appeared on the front page of Nanfang Ribao the next day (NFRB, 10 February 1965). In March Zhao "squatted" in Zhongshan xian (see text). By April he was back in Guangzhou where he appeared at the Beijing opera performance of Surprise Attack on White Tiger Regiment (NFRB, 11 April 1965). In June Zhao attended, addressed, and was elected chairman of the Guangdong Poor and Lower-Middle Peasants' Association Conference (YCWB, 15 and 25 June 1965). During June he also met with recent college graduates (YCMB, 12 June 1965) and attended more musical performances (YCWB, 24 June and 5 July 1965). In July Zhao attended the opening of the Central-South Drama Festival (RMRB, 2 July 1965), met with a Vietnamese delegation (RMRB, 5 July 1965), and held a forum with rural mobile medical teams (YCWB, 21 July 1965). In August Zhao met with Guangzhou militiamen on Army Day (YCWB, 1 August 1965), met with representatives of the Third Guangdong Students' Conference (YCWB, 10 August 1965), met Japanese Communist Party leaders (RMRB, 15 August 1965), and delivered an "important report" to the Guangdong Meeting of Activists to Exchange Experiences in Studying Mao's Works (YCWB, 30 August 1965, see text). In September Zhao met another visiting Vietnamese delegation (NCNA, Guangzhou, 9 September 1965) and attended the Guangdong "Five-Good" and Advanced Representatives in Industry, Communications, Finance and Trade Conference (NFRB, 27 September 1965). In October he met yet another Vietnamese delegation (RMRB, 1 November 1965). In December Zhao attended the Third Session of the Third Guangdong People's Congress (NFRB, 21 December 1965) and received overseas Chinese observers to the congress (YCWB, 24 December 1965).

4
Losing Power:
The Cultural Revolution, 1966–1968

Zhao had reached the pinnacle of provincial political power, but he stood to lose it all. Within a year, Zhao would go from the privileged life of first Party secretary to public humiliation and internal exile. At the beginning of 1966 such a fate was impossible to fathom.

During the first seven months of 1966, Zhao offered no indication of uneasiness. He continued on in his duties as usual. He appeared regularly and encouraged various groups to intensify the campaign to study Mao's works.[1] In March and April Zhao made an inspection tour of Hainan Island and Dongfang xian. While visiting the latter, he gave a speech to local cadres titled "Thoroughly Remold Your World Outlook." In it, Zhao exhorted:

> We are revolutionaries. Revolution is aimed at changing a backward society and changing a backward production level. Therefore, the greater the difficulties involved in a place and the more backward it is, the greater is the need for us to make revolution there. The more backward a place, the more there is to do. Courage in struggling with heaven and earth, with mankind and with difficulties and backwardness is a source of the greatest joy to a revolutionary (emphasis added).[2]

Here we see Zhao defining revolution in terms of raising production. This is not unusual for him, but how did he propose to raise output? Zhao had this to say:

> Production along the revisionist line has as its prop material incentives. In our socialist revolution and construction, the most fundamental factor we rely upon is bringing politics to the fore and raising the people's consciousness. This is an objective demand imposed by the laws governing the development of socialism and by the socialist economic foundation. Many facts show that if the

consciousness of the people and especially of the cadres is raised, backward areas will very quickly become advanced ones.[3]

Thus in this speech we see Zhao advocating his familiar production theme, but rather than advocating material incentives he endorses Mao's voluntarist emphasis on human consciousness as the means to transform the economic base. This reveals Zhao's opportunist character, which became manifest when there were changing policy lines at the center. When in doubt, agree with the Chairman.

With the issuance of Mao's 16 May 1966 Circular, a new impetus was given to a chain reaction of events, begun the previous November, that would shake China's polity and society to the core. The Cultural Revolution was brewing. This was an extremely complex event about which many volumes have been written. For our purposes, we will limit the discussion to those events at the center which directly affected Zhao Ziyang and Zhao's personal behavior and fate during the movement.

The 16 May Circular affected Zhao because it called for the removal of, among others, Lu Dingyi, who was director of the CCP Propaganda Department. Lu was purged in early June and replaced by none other than Tao Zhu. Before the year was out, Tao would become the fourth highest-ranking official in the nation (behind Mao, Zhou Enlai, and Lin Biao). Zhao had reason to feel secure; he had a patron at the highest echelons of central leadership. Tao brought to Beijing four notable aides from the Central-South Bureau: Wang Renzhong, Zhang Pinghua, Yong Wentao, and Zeng Zhi (his wife).[4] Zhao was left behind where he served concurrently as general secretary of the Central-South Bureau's Secretariat and first Party secretary of Guangdong. Therefore Tao Zhu could also feel secure with provincial affairs in the hands of his trusted colleague. Tao's promotion has been attributed to his close relationship with both Lin Biao and Deng Xiaoping.[5] In addition to taking over the important post of director of the Propaganda Department, Tao was also charged by Liu Shaoqi with overseeing the dissemination of work teams to the provinces during the hectic "Fifty Days."[6] Like Liu, Tao did his best to use the work teams as a stabilizing force, i.e., to pursue "closed-door" investigation and rectification.[7] True, their orders were to "sweep out all monsters and ghosts," but in most cases this meant that a few individuals in a given unit of a Party committee would be criticized. Frequently these individuals had previously been labeled as "rightists" in 1957. On 22 June Tao Zhu reportedly telephoned Zhao from Beijing concerning "power seizures" in schools.[8] Tao instructed Zhao to keep the work teams then going into schools strictly under the control and supervision of the provincial CCP committee. All student mobilization must be controlled by these work teams, which may include members of the Communist Youth League. Tao also reportedly told

Zhao to beware of power seizures by "enemies with leftist features." For his part, Zhao appears to have followed these orders during the Fifty Days. In late June he was reported to have convened a meeting of all Guangzhou work team leaders and instructed them that the movement would be directed against the "power holders" in schools rather than teachers, who had been unfairly labeled as "monsters and ghosts."[9] However, in fact, these work teams often protected the Party committees and suppressed the students who attacked them.[10]

After swimming the Yangzi River to demonstrate his fitness, Mao returned to Beijing and, in early August, convened the Eleventh Plenum of the Eighth Central Committee. While this watershed meeting was taking place, Zhao convened his own conference in Guangzhou on agricultural mechanization in experimental communes.[11] As in the past, Zhao was not going to allow this campaign to interfere with the upcoming fall harvest. The Eleventh Plenum was a major turning point in the unfolding Cultural Revolution. It represented the ascendancy of the Cultural Revolution Small Group (CRSG) and radical Red Guards, and the concomitant decline in power of Liu Shaoqi and the conservative Red Guards. Liu Shaoqi was severely criticized by Mao for his handling of the work teams during the Fifty Days and was demoted from second to eighth place in the Central Committee hierarchy. Lin Biao replaced him as vice-chairman of the Central Committee. Other personnel changes included expansion of the Politburo to thirty-two members, with Tao Zhu, Kang Sheng, and Chen Boda being made members of the Standing Committee. With this "packing" of the leadership with more leftist elements, Mao was able to push through the adoption of the "Sixteen Articles" at the Plenum. Among other things, this document officially sanctioned the Red Guards to "struggle against the power holders taking the capitalist road within the Party." The stage was now set for the rapid expansion of the campaign.

On 5 August Mao made his famous call to the Red Guards at Beijing University to "bombard the headquarters." Red Guards from the capital began to fan out to all major cities to instruct local Red Guard organizations on how to proceed with the movement. The Great Proletarian Cultural Revolution was gaining momentum.

Immediately following the Eleventh Plenum, Tao Zhu telephoned Zhao and urged him to move forcefully to avoid being overtaken by the rush of events and to retain control over the rising activism in middle schools and universities.[12] Zhao did his best to stem the tide by meeting with Red Guard leaders from Guangzhou middle schools. For example, he called into his office the leader of the Huafu Rebels from the "East is Red" (Dongfanghong) middle school (whose student body included several children of high-level provincial officials) to try and persuade him not to put up a poster at the school which called for "bombarding the provincial Party committee."[13] Zhao's effort failed; the poster was put up and the infamous "Huafu Eleven" were born. Zhao also addressed rallies of various conservative Red Guard groups in Guangzhou on 1, 3, and 17 September and congratulated them on their successful "smashing of the four olds" (old ideology, thought, habits, and customs).[14] As several groups of conservative Red Guards dispatched from the center began to pour into the province throughout August, Zhao opportunistically published a lengthy article in Hongqi titled "Energetically Launch the Mass Campaign for Studying Chairman Mao's Writings, Speed Up the Proletarian Revolutionization of Peasants' Thought." As the title indicates, Zhao's article emphasized the dissemination of the Chairman's works in the countryside. Its content closely parallels Zhao's August 1965 speech. For example, his discussion of the relationship between politics and production is almost identical.

> In studying Chairman Mao's works how should our priorities be arranged? Or it can be said, should politics or production have precedence? What are these sayings we hear: "if production is good, then politics will be good," "production cannot wait overnight, politics can wait until next year," "production prevails over everything," "if production is good, you can hide ugliness," "politics is important, production is also important," "a poor harvest is due to politics, a good harvest is due to production," "politics should serve production, otherwise it is a new flower growing in the road," etc.? The effect of this kind of bourgeois thinking on our cadres' thinking cannot be underestimated, it is a critical situation. If we do not use Mao Zedong Thought as our commander, then all of our work will be for naught, we will lose our direction, and we will not be able to equip ourselves with liberated thinking. Concerning the problem of the relationship between politics and production, if we do not decide to study Chairman Mao's works in earnest, raise our intensity, combat the bourgeois class, correctly identify revisionism, then capitalism will certainly be restored, and we will sink into the morass of revisionism."[15]

Zhao also contributed to Mao's personality cult with repeated sycophantic quotes and references to the Chairman's "invincible" thought. Zhao also praised Lin Biao and the exemplary job the PLA had done in the "flexible application" of Mao's works. Lastly, Zhao dwelled on the most recent stage of the SEM, i.e., to "smash the four olds." His article does not, however, mention Mao's call to "bombard the headquarters," the events of the "Fifty Days," or any of the stipulations set forth in the Eleventh Plenum communique or the "Sixteen Articles." These omissions are probably due to the fact that Zhao's article was written, and went to press, before these events of early August. Nevertheless, the strong ideological tenor of the article was a stark departure from the majority of Zhao's earlier speeches and writings. This article bought Zhao a little time, but not much. The momemtum of the Cultural Revolution was increasing daily.

The Cultural Revolution was given added impetus, and lurched sharply leftward, in early October with Lin Biao's National Day speech, the 3 October Hongqi editorial, the 5 October "Urgent Directive" of the Military Commission and PLA General Political Department, and the 6 October rally in Tian'anmen square. How did Zhao respond to these documents? First, he issued a call for all college and middle school students and teachers to go immediately to the countryside to "exchange experiences" (chuanlian) with peasants and to help "save" the fall harvest.[16] Thus, true to form, Zhao was putting production first. But this tactic (which was only partially successful) also would get the Red Guards out of Guangzhou and would therefore take the pressure off Zhao and the provincial Party committee. Second, upon Tao Zhu's instruction, Zhao and the committee switched support from the conservative to the radical Red Guard factions.[17] But in so doing the Party committee did not attempt to destroy the conservative faction. Rather, it instructed them to accept the "switch of direction" and to disperse to the countryside, chuanlian, and help with the harvest and drought relief.[18] In this way they could lie low and wait for the proper opportunity to assert themselves. Third, on Tao Zhu's urging, Zhao made a public self-criticism on behalf of the entire provincial Party committee on 4 November.[19] These efforts to buy time and defuse the movement did not work. The radical Red Guards had gained enough strength and momentum to seize the initiative in their hands. To be sure, as the research of Hong Yung Lee and Stanley Rosen demonstrates,[20] at this point in time the Red Guards were far from being a cohesive lot but they nevertheless had the imprimatur of the CRSG in Beijing.

Pressure was not only increasing on Zhao in Guangzhou, but also on Tao Zhu in Beijing. Tao, now the first-ranking "advisor" to the CRSG, was in a very precarious position. Many conservative leaders with whom he had been affiliated at various times in his career were being "knocked down" and "dragged out" for public ridicule. On 7 November Tao himself came under attack in wall posters for the first time in Beijing. By 20 November the wall poster attacks on Tao had spread to Guangzhou. Needless to say, this undermined his continuing efforts to keep control of the Red Guards going south. The new Red Guard arrivals in Guangzhou in December now spearheaded the campaign against Tao Zhu and immediately attempted to seize control of Yangcheng Wanbao which they considered to be Tao's mouthpiece in Guangdong. Tao telephoned Zhao and other provincial officials and ordered them not to oppose the takeover.[21] They acquiesced and a confrontation was avoided. Also in December, in an opportunistic attempt to save himself, Tao became the first high official to attack Liu

Shaoqi and Deng Xiaoping publicly by name, but tried to limit the attacks on them by claiming that their cases belonged to "contradictions among the people."[22] Even this tactic was not enough to save Tao, and on 4 January 1967, he was named a "counterrevolutionary double-dealer" by the CRSG. The next day Guangzhou was covered with posters criticizing him. The way was now cleared to criticize Zhao. The following day, 6 January, Zhao was attacked in a Beijing Red Guard tabloid for "taking the capitalist road and stubbornly adhering to the bourgeois reactionary line, and having been protected by Tao Zhu, Wang Renzhong, and Zhang Pinghua."[23] On 15 January Zhao came under attack in Guangzhou for having been Tao Zhu's henchman.[24] Having been Zhao's superior and patron for fifteen years, the two men's fates were inextricably linked together. Just as they had risen together, they would now fall from power together.

With the 1 January People's Daily editorial urging the Red Guards to band together and to "seize power," the pressure on the Guangdong Party committee mounted. A multitude of disparate Red Guard organizations merged into the Provincial Revolutionary Alliance (sheng ge lian). On 16 January the Alliance issued an ultimatum to the provincial Party committee to prepare for a transfer of power to the rebels.

The events of the 22 January "power seizure" are very complex. The most thorough description of these events is contained in statements supposedly made by Zhao and Lin Liming two weeks after the fact.[25] Zhao's personal description of the power seizure includes the following. On the afternoon of 21 January Zhao attended a meeting with representatives of the Alliance at the Guangdong CCP committee's Party school. The purpose of the meeting was to criticize the committee's bourgeois reactionary line. When the meeting disbanded, Zhao was told to climb on the back of a flat-bed "propaganda truck" where he joined Ou Mengjue and two others. They were taken to the Hongqi (Red Flag) commune at Zhongshan University.[26] Zhao was interrogated there until midnight. At six o'clock in the morning of the twenty-second, Zhao was read an order by Red Guards for the seizure of power, and they demanded that he forthwith turn over the "chops" (seals) of the Guangdong CCP Committee, the General Office, and the Cultural Revolution Office. Zhao thereupon wrote a note to Lin Liming instructing him to turn over the seals to the Red Guards. The students then proceeded to the provincial CCP committee headquarters to find Lin. Lin's account of the days' events (contained in the same Red Guard source) states that when the students arrived he claimed that he did not possess the authority to turn over the seals, despite Zhao's instructions to do so. Lin suggested that this decision must be made by the entire Secretariat. The students rejected this idea, and Lin then proceeded to call the General Office of the CCP Central Committee in Beijing for instructions. His call was put through, but he was told that "the responsible comrade was not in the office," and he would be called back. After the call, Lin was taken to Zhongshan University to join Zhao and the others, where he informed Zhao of his call to Beijing and suggested that the Party center (dang zhongyang) be asked for approval before turning over the seals.

After lengthy discussion, it was decided that since a reply from Beijing might not be immediately forthcoming, the seals should be turned over pending the request to Beijing for instructions. Consequently, the following document was drafted and signed.

Agreement of the Use of Seals

The Secretariat of the provincial committee (some comrades are absent) decides that the Great Seal of the provincial committee should be frozen (temporarily), that the seals of the General Office and the Office for the Cultural Revolution should be used under the supervision of the Alliance, that the Great Seal of the provincial committee should be supervised by the Alliance, and that they should all be removed to another place. The above-mentioned seals can be used only with the approval of the supervisors designated by the Alliance. The key (to the receptacle holding the seals) shall be in the hands of the persons designated by the Alliance.

	(Signed)	Zhao Ziyang
		Lin Liming
		Ou Mengjue
January 22		Zhang Yun[27]

Not included in the document, but agreed to by the Alliance, according to Zhao's supposed account, is the fact that the Red Guards instructed the Secretariat of the provincial Party committee to continue to "carry out its work properly" under their supervision. This decision was affirmed at a meeting of the Secretariat on the afternoon of the twenty-second at an enlarged Standing Committee meeting in the evening, and in a "public notice" issued the following day.[28] Zhao and his colleagues were permitted for the time being to live at home and work at the East Wing No. 1 building. According to Lin Liming's account, after the seizure of power Premier Zhou Enlai telephoned his approval of the takeover and ordered the PLA Military District Command to maintain order if necessary.

On 25 February Tao, Zhao, Ou, Lin, and others were paraded through the streets with dunce caps on their heads and placards around their necks, subjected to several mass criticism sessions, and then disappeared from public view.[29] Tao was never to be seen in public again, and Zhao disappeared from the public eye until 16 October 1967 when he, Ou Mengjue, and

Yin Linping were "dragged out" before a mass criticism session of 80,000 people at Yuexiushan square in Guangzhou.[30] Zhao was not seen again in public for three and a half years, although he would continue to be ridiculed in the Guangdong press until July 1968.

The charges brought against Zhao were numerous. I believe that the most systematic way to inventory them is to present the charges chronologically as Zhao's career developed. During the formation of mutual aid teams in 1953, Zhao was accused, along with Tao Zhu, of:

— ignoring the central directive "Resolution on Mutual Aid and Cooperation," on the grounds that Guangdong was designated a "new area." Not a single cooperative was established until 1953.[31]

During the movement to transform mutual aid teams (MATs) into lower agricultural producer cooperatives (LAPCs) in 1955-1956, Zhao was accused of:

— being a member of the "get off the horse faction" (xiama pai), being an apologist for rich peasants, and opposing the transformation of MATs into LAPCs.[32]

During the Great Leap Forward Zhao was accused of:

— suppressing the movement to study Chairman Mao's works in the Guangdong countryside;[33]

— concealing production figures in Xuwen xian in 1959;[34]

— submitting false production figures to the center;[35]

— being a member of the "three-anti" clique (anti-Mao, anti-socialism, and anti-CCP);[36]

— pushing revisionist agricultural and economic policies for the purposes of disintegrating the people's communes and restoring capitalism during 1959-1960;[37]

— watching pornographic movies (huangse dianying) in the provincial Party committee headquarters during 1959-1961.[38]

During the post-Great Leap recovery (1960-1962), Zhao was accused of:

— promoting agricultural policies which included the sanzi yibao, giving cash bonuses to over-producers, and advocating self-management;[39]

— using Zhouxin and Nanzhong communes in Jingyuan xian as models of the "responsibility system of field management";[40]

— colluding with class enemies at home and abroad in opposing the "three red banners";[41]

— suggesting a "coordination of three powers" (the power of the Party, the power of the government, and the power of technology).[42]

During the Socialist Education Movement (1962-1965), Zhao was accused of:

— attempting to cover up the Shengshi brigade incident in 1964 after he had promoted it as a model for the whole province to emulate (Zhao's relationship with Chen Hua, the Party secretary of the brigade, dated back to 1956);[43]

— failing to implement Mao's "Twenty Three Articles";[44]

— distorting the "Four Clean-ups" movement to mean "construction for production" in his article "Building the Comparatively Poor Countryside into an Affluent New Socialist Countryside";[45]

— advocating the "theory of the extinction of class struggle" and claiming that class contradictions were contradictions "among the people";[46]

— promoting "economism" along with Liu Shaoqi, Deng Xiaoping, and Chen Yun;[47]

— suppressing a letter from the people of Henan province which alleged some serious mistakes made by Zhao's wife;[48]

— harboring Liu Shaoqi and Wang Guangmei during their 1964 visit and peddling their "black line" of the "Taoyuan Experience."[49]

During the buildup to the Cultural Revolution in 1966, Zhao was accused of:

— suppressing the "letter from Beijing" wall poster at the South China Engineering College and ordering the Public Security Bureau to harass its authors;[50]

— disobeying the instructions of Chen Boda after the Eleventh Plenum by advocating the "clearing of accounts after the autumn harvest";[51]

— promoting the "black wind of economism" in Maoming municipality in August and September;[52]

— double-dealing in his September 1966 _Hongqi_ article;[53]

— dispatching numerous work teams to suppress Red Guards during the Fifty Days. Then in September 1966 he tried to coopt the leaders of various Red Guard groups. When this effort failed he tried to infiltrate them by organizing "liaison departments" in order to foster a "royalist force." When this did not work he attempted to bribe students with automobiles, bicycles, and broadcast equipment. For this purpose, he even sent special personnel to Shanghai by plane to purchase parts for making transistor radio receivers. In these efforts to bribe and corrupt student organizations he squandered a total of 578,000 yuan;[54]

— attempting to insulate research institutes from the Cultural Revolution;[55]

— refusing to criticize Liu Shaoqi and Deng Xiaoping in November;[56]

— trying to form an "iron block" to protect his own gang of Ou Mengjue, Zhang Yun, Wang Kuang, Wang Lanxi, and Chen Yueping;[57]

— convening a secret meeting to draw up a "unified scheme," after Tao Zhu was criticized, and burning "blacklist information to destroy the damning evidence";[58]

— manipulating the Nanfang Ribao editors to support conservative Red Guards;[59]

— attacking, opposing, and refusing to implement Chen Boda's report to the November 1967 CCP Central Committee work conference on "Two Lines in the Great Proletarian Revolution";[60]

— denying that he had taken the capitalist road a day after the January power seizure, and claiming that he was to supervise the Provincial Revolutionary Alliance.[61]

These are the most significant charges leveled against Zhao Ziyang by Red Guards after his fall from power in January 1967. One other Red Guard accusation merits mention. In February 1968, Zhao is reported to have written a 10,000 character self-criticism which, as might be expected, was denounced as an attempt to "reverse the verdict" on himself and launch the so-called "February adverse current."[62] After writing his self-criticism, Zhao reportedly asked Huang Yongsheng (the Guangzhou Military Region commander who was in de facto control of Guangdong at this time) to petition Mao and the CRSG on his behalf and ask for a reconsideration of his case. Huang reportedly granted the request, but Zhao's petition for rehabilitation was turned down by Mao.[63] Huang then reportedly ordered Nanfang Ribao to publish the following article on 26 April 1968 attacking Zhao's self-criticism. The actual text of Zhao's self-criticism is not available, but the Nanfang Ribao critique included several purported quotations. For example, Zhao is quoted as having written:

In the past seventeen years since Liberation, at practically every critical moment when a storm arises, I have always followed Tao Zhu in carrying out the Liu-Deng reactionary line and in upsetting Chairman Mao's revolutionary line from the right or extreme left. . . . I lost my bearings and did not realize this was a struggle between two lines. . . . The reason why I have made so many grave mistakes is that I have very poorly studied Chairman Mao's writings and his instructions, and I have not made a serious effort to study them. When trying to solve problems, I have either forgotten Chairman Mao's teachings or completely been in the dark. Whenever I do not understand them or find them unacceptable to my own way of thinking, I do not closely follow them and firmly implement them. Often I am inclined to give undue emphasis to certain portions of Chairman Mao's instructions that correspond to my thinking. . . . Being seriously rightist-inclined and conservative, I have merely observed rich peasant's lack of confidence in the cooperativization movement, not the potentially abundant enthusiasm for socialism on the part of the broad masses of poor and lower-middle peasants. . . . In the face of certain difficulties and setbacks, I began to incline to the right and waver, even pushing the revolution backward. During the period of temporary economic difficulties, I made a number of rightist-inclined mistakes . . . all being manifestations of doubt toward the socialist collective economy in rural areas. . . . By seeking immediate results, and not giving consideration to fundamental, long-range political consequences, I adopted the attitude of a pragmatist who tried to act wisely by thinking out some petty measures and ideas."[64]

The article further querried,

Has Zhao Ziyang really mended his his ways? No he has not. Instead, he has continued to resist and defy the orders issued by the proletarian headquarters and continued to carry out in different disguises the bourgeois reactionary line espoused by China's Khrushchev. . . . In his "examination" Zhao Ziyang pretended to express his deep remorse and to make amends with resolution, but in an utterly cunning way denied he was a capitalist-roader in power and denied he ever committed towering crimes against the Party, against socialism, and against the Thought of Mao Zedong. Was Zhao Ziyang really repentant after all? No, he merely bared his sinister motives which were behind his intrigues to reverse the correct verdict on him and to stage a comeback. He also revealed his deep-seated hatred of his mallicious intentions to slander others

60

and his frenzied efforts to strike back! Zhao Ziyang is a capitalist-roader, this being epitomized in his own counterrevolutionary background over the past decades, particularly in the past seventeen years since Liberation.[65]

NOTES

1. In January Zhao attended a reception for overseas Chinese (Renmin Ribao, hereafter RMRB, 20 January 1966). In February he met with local-level cadres of Haikou city and encouraged them to study Mao's works (Yangcheng Wanbao, hereafter YCWB, 2 March 1966). In April Zhao met with a Japanese Communist Party delegation (Renmin Ribao, hereafter RMRB, 5 April 1966) and saw Vice-Premier Li Xiannian off to Cambodia (RMRB, 25 April 1966). In May he received medical personnel going to the countryside (YCWB, 6 May 1966) and delivered a report on politics and law to the Congress of "Four Good" Units and "Five Good" Cadres in the People's Police (Radio Guangzhou, 30 May 1966). In June Zhao addressed the Third Enlarged Session of the Guangdong Communist Youth League provincial committee (Radio Guangzhou, 22 June 1966) and made an aerial inspection of the East River area floods (Radio Guangzhou, 23 June 1966). In July Zhao attended two anti-American/pro-Vietnamese rallies (RMRB, 12 and 24 July 1966).

2. YCWB, 30 March 1966; translated in Survey Mainland China Press (hereafter SCMP), No. 3674, 7 April 1966, pp. 1-3.

3. Ibid.

4. For an account of these individuals and why Tao chose them, see "Remove the Mask of Tao Zhu as a 'Proletarian Revolutionary,' " Jinggangshan, 11 January 1967, translated in Current Background (hereafter CB), No. 825, 1967.

5. See Peter R. Moody, Jr., "Power and Policy: The Career of Tao Zhu, 1956-66," in China Quarterly, No. 54 (1973).

6. Ibid., Ezra Vogel, Canton Under Communism (Cambridge, 2d ed., 1980), p. 325.

7. For Liu's role, see Lowell Dittmer, Liu Shao-ch'i and the Cultural Revolution: The Politics of Mass Criticism (Berkeley, 1974).

8. "Tao Zhu Is the Khrushchev of Central-South China," CB, No. 824, 27 April 1967.

9. Gordon Bennett and Ronald Monteperto, Red Guard: The Political Biography of Dai Hsiao-ai (New York, 1971), p. 52.

10. Hong Yung Lee, The Politics of the Chinese Cultural Revolution (Berkeley, 1978), p. 229.

11. Radio Guangzhou, 3 August 1966, as reported in News from Chinese Regional Radio Stations, No. 169, 11 August 1966, p. 30.

12. CB, No. 824, p. 47; Communist China Digest, No. 191, pp. 68-71; China News Analysis, No. 724 (6 September 1968); as cited in Vogel, Canton Under Communism, p. 327.

13. Stanley Rosen, Red Guard Factionalism and the Cultural Revolution in Guangzhou (Boulder, 1982), p. 173.

14. Gordon Bennett and Ronald Monteperto, Red Guard, p. 84; Hong Wei Bao (Guangzhou), 3 September 1966; News from Chinese Provincial Radio Stations, No. 175, 22 September 1966, p. 30; ibid., No. 172, 1 September 1966, p. 34.

15. Hongqi (Red Flag), No. 10, 10 August 1966, pp. 24-25.

16. Bennett and Monteperto, Red Guard, p. 107.

17. Lee, The Politics of the Cultural Revolution, p. 230.

18. Ibid.

19. Vogel, Canton Under Communism. No text or report of the self-criticism is available.

20. Lee, The Politics of the Cultural Revolution; Rosen, Red Guard Factionalism; Stanley Rosen, "The Radical Students in Guangdong During the Cultural Revolution," China Quarterly, No. 70 (June 1977), pp. 390-99; and Lee, "A Reply," ibid., pp. 399-406.

21. "The True Face of Tao Zhu," Survey of Mainland China Magazines (hereafter SCMM), 1 May 1967, pp. 20-27.

22. Moody, "Power and Policy: The Career of Tao Zhu, 1956-66." It should be noted that Mao had done the same in October.

23. "Tao Zhu Is an Out-and-Out Royalist," Shoudu Hongweibing (Capital Red Guard), 6 January 1967, p. 3.

24. "Thirty Four Whys," Hongse Zao Fanzhe (Red Rebels), No. 3, 15 January 1967, translated in SCMP, No. 3915, pp. 5-8.

25. "Facts of the 'January 22' Seizure of Power," Guangzhou Hongweibing (Guangzhou Red Guards), 10 February 1967, translated in SCMP, No. 3929, 1 May 1967.

26. This description of the events of 21 January do not correspond to Dai Xiao'ai's account in Bennett and Monteperto's Red Guard. Dai claims that when representatives of the Alliance went to provincial CCP headquarters to demand that Zhao turn over the "chops" of the committee, Zhao was not there. They found him later in the day at the Agricultural and Forestry Bureau, and then took him to Zhongshan University.

27. Guangzhou Hongweibing, 10 February 1967; translated in SCMP, No. 3929, 1 May 1967.

28. "Message from the Guangdong CCP Committee to All Party Members, Cadres, and People of the Province," Guangzhou Hongweibing, 10 February 1967, translated in SCMP, No. 3929, pp. 12-15.

29. Interviews with two eyewitnesses confirmed this (June 1982).

30. Guangdong Ke-Ji Zhan Bao (Guangdong Science and Technology Combat Bulletin), 25 October 1967, translated in SCMP, No. 4059, 14 November 1967.

31. Fan Xiu Zhan Bao (Anti-Revisionist Combat Bulletin), 8 July 1967, translated in SCMP, No. 4018, 11 September 1967.

32. Shengzhi Hongqi (Provincial Organization Red Flag), No. 5 (January 1968), pp. 1,4; as reported in Red Guard Press (hereafter RGP), compiled by the Center for Chinese Research Materials (Washington, D.C.), Vol. 11, pp. 3458, 3461.

33. Xiao Bing (Little Soldier), 25 February 1967, p. 4; translated in Union Research Service (hereafter URS), Vol. 47, p. 225.

34. Hongse Zao Fanzhe, 4 January 1968, pp. 1-4; RGP, Vol. 7, pp. 1985-86.

35. Fan Xiu Zhan Bao, 8 July 1967.

36. Ibid.

37. "Zhao Ziyang's Eight Major Misdeeds," in Nianqing Zhanshi (Young Fighters), 25 February 1967, translated in SCMM, No. 575 (April 1967).

38. Xinwen Zhance (Journalism Warrior), RGP, Vol. 6, p. 1462.

39. Nianqing Zhanshi, 25 February 1967.

40. Xiao Bing, 25 February 1967; Fan Xiu Zhan Bao, 8 July 1967.

41. Ibid., p. 226.

42. Hongqi Ruhua (Red Flag Unfurled Like a Scroll), No. 1 (January 1968), p. 1; RGP, Vol. 6, p. 1681.

43. San Zhan Bao (Third War Bulletin), No. 30 (15 June 1967); RGP, Vol. 11, p. 3416.

44. Ye Zhan Bao (Open Warfare Bulletin), No. 10 (31 October 1967).

45. Ibid.

46. Guangzhou Gong Dai Hui (Guangzhou Workers Representative Conference), No. 3, 18 March 1968, p. 3; RGP, Vol. 9, p. 2665.

47. Xiao Bing, 25 February 1967.

48. Ibid.

49. Ye Zhan Bao, 31 October 1967.

50. Hongqi Bao (Red Flag Bulletin), No. 29, 24 June 1967, translated in SCMP, No. 4026, 22 September 1967.

51. Hongqi Ruhua, No. 1, January 1968.

52. Kuangbiao (Wild Whirlwind), 11 January 1968, translated in SCMP, No. 4119, 15 February 1968.

53. Zhong Da Zhan Bao (Zhongshan University War Bulletin), No. 47, 14 April 1968, pp. 2-4; RGP, Vol. 4, pp. 0835-37.

54. Xiao Bing, 25 February 1967; Ye Zhan Bao, 31 October 1967.

55. Yi Yue Feng Bao (January Storm), January 1968, p. 3; RGP, Vol. 8, p. 2387.

56. Xiao Bing, 25 February 1967.

57. Ibid., p. 231.

58. Ye Zhan Bao, 31 October 1967.

59. Zhandou Wei Yi (Militant Literature and Art), No. 4, June 1968, translated in SCMM, No. 629, 30 September 1968.

60. Hongqi Ruhua, No. 1, January 1968.

61. Xiao Bing, 25 February 1967.

62. Zhong Da Hongqi (Zhongshan University Red Flag), No. 66, 26 April 1968, p. 4; RGP, Vol. 4, p. 0874; Ji Da Gelian (Jinan University Revolutionary Alliance), No. 4, 28 April 1968, p. 2; RGP, Vol. 2, p. 0140; Zhan Guangdong (Fighting Guangdong), 10 July 1968, translated in SCMM, No. 629, 30 September 1968.

63. Ibid; "Zhao Ziyang's Record," Dang Dai (Hong Kong), 15 February 1981, p. 18.

64. "Expose a Big Plot to Strike Back Under the Pretext of Making a 'Self-Examination,' Exposing 'My Examination' by Zhao Ziyang, the Top Party Capitalist-Roader in Guangdong," NFRB, 26 April 1968, translated in SCMP, No. 4185, 24 May 1968, pp. 1-9.

65. Ibid.

5
Rehabilitation and Return
to Guangdong, 1971–1975

After failing to have his "verdict reversed" in 1968, Zhao completely dropped from public view for more than three years. On 22 May 1971 he resurfaced and was identified as a Party secretary in Inner Mongolia.[1] What was Zhao doing at the opposite end of the country, some 2,000 kilometers from Guangdong, his name last on a list of provincial officials of the Inner Mongolian Autonomous Region? Where had he been for three years? These questions cannot be conclusively answered because corroborative evidence is lacking. However, knowledgeable Chinese who worked with Zhao in Guangdong before and after the Cultural Revolution claim that he spent the entire period at a remote May Seventh Cadre School (wuqi ganxiao) in Inner Mongolia.[2] Actually, being exiled to Inner Mongolia may have been a blessing in disguise. That is, he was more isolated and insulated from rampaging Red Guards and the excesses of the Cultural Revolution. Those leaders who were detained in interior provinces bore the brunt of persecution. Many died, some of them by their own hand, others at the hands of Red Guards and/or jailers (including Zhao's patron, Tao Zhu, who died of cancer in prison in 1969). Knowledgeable Chinese also claim that Zhou Enlai did his best to protect cadres loyal to him by having them assigned, for their own protection, to May Seventh schools away from the interior. Similarly, Zhou also probably played an important role in Zhao's rehabilitation. Whatever the reasons for Zhao's fate during this period, he was rehabilitated and quickly climbed the ladder of provincial power. By January 1972 Zhao was identified as vice-chairman of the Inner Mongolian Autonomous Region Revolutionary Committee. In eight months he had risen from the least important to the second most important provincial official. However, he was not to stay in the north much longer.

In March 1972 Zhao was transferred back to Guangdong, and he publicly appeared in Guangzhou during April to meet delegations from Mauritius and Afghanistan, and was identified as vice-chairman of the Guangdong Provincial Revolutionary Committee. Zhao continued to be identified in this post throughout the year when he met with delegations from Sierra Leone in May, from Kuwait in July, from Canada in August, from Tunisia in September, from Nepal in November, and welcomed foreign businessmen to the Canton Trade Fair in October.[3]

One can only speculate on who or what was responsible for Zhao's rapid rise in Inner Mongolia during the latter half of 1971 and for his transfer back to Guangdong, but it is a reasonable assumption that it was related to the erosion of Lin Biao's power base throughout the first half of 1971 and his death following a supposed coup d'etat attempt in September.[4] During this period many of Lin's provincial allies (mostly former Fourth Field Army personnel) were replaced by military personnel (mostly of Second and Third Field Army backgrounds) and rehabilitated Party cadres who were more responsive to Mao Zedong and Zhou Enlai.[5] Thus Zhao's rehabilitation and transfer back to Guangdong ought to be viewed as part of a national pattern of personnel changes following the Lin Biao affair. However, returning Zhao to his home base was not tantamount to his being restored to power. The political landscape had changed considerably during his absence. This is a long and intricate story which has been dealt with elsewhere.[6] Suffice it to say here that Zhao still had to contend with those who were responsible for his original fall from power, namely, military allies of Huang Yongsheng and former members of the Red Flag faction of Red Guards, which together composed the bulk of the reconstituted Guangdong Revolutionary Committee.

Zhao's only public appearance in the first eight months of 1973 was at the Canton Trade Fair in April.[7] Zhao reappeared in August 1973 in Beijing at the Tenth CCP Congress, where he was elected a member of the Presidium of the congress and, for the first time in his career, was made a member of the Central Committee. He was also identified in the provincial posts of secretary of the Guangdong CCP committee and vice-chairman of the Revolutionary Committee. Following the congress, Zhao continued to be absent from public view until 1974. After the new year, Zhao began to reassert his active and visible work style. He resumed meeting with foreign dignitaries as they passed through Guangdong, though they now were no longer merely leaders of obscure Communist parties and Third World nations but some Western heads of state as well. For example, in 1974 alone, Zhao hosted Bristish Prime Minister Edward Heath, Danish Prime Minister Vance Hartling, Zambian President Kenneth Kaunda, Tanzanian President Julius Nyerere, Cyriot President Makarios, Gabonese President Abbot Bongo, Zairian President Joseph Mobutu, the Austrian Communist Party chairman, and delegations from North Vietnam and South Yemen. This sample is quite representative of the multiple emphases in Chinese foreign policy at the time. Zhao also began to show up at a number of army-related gatherings, probably in an attempt to cultivate alliances with the PLA, which itself had been cast in a more important political position in the reconstituted Revolutionary Committees. In addition to his involvement in military and foreign affairs, Zhao became quite active in a variety of issue areas other than agriculture, his long-cultivated specialty. The public record notes his presence at conferences dealing with ideological affairs (e.g., the Criticize Lin Biao and Confucius and Dictatorship of the Proletariat Campaigns), militia work, trade unions, sports, birth control, women, youth, performing arts, literature, health care, law, industry, foreign trade, science and technology. The brief examination of his major speeches during 1974 and 1975 below highlights Zhao's involvement in diversified issue areas and allows us to evaluate whether or not his positions on issues had changed as a result of his Cultural Revolution experience.

Zhao gave two major speeches on agriculture in 1974. The language and content of these speeches is very different from his agriculture speeches of the pre-Cultural Revolution era. His language was more rhetorical and the content was more propagandistic and less substantive. Nevertheless, his basic goal remained increased production even though his methods had changed rather dramatically. For example, in a speech to a provincial rural work conference in June 1974, he explicitly attacked "Liu Shaoqi's counterrevolutionary revisionist policies of material incentives, the sanzi yibao, and the four great freedoms" (freedom of usury, of hiring labor, land sale, and private enterprise).[8] Similarly, in December 1974 in a lengthy speech to the Second Guangdong Congress of the Poor and Lower-Middle Peasants Association, Zhao extolled the virtues of the Dazhai model of agricultural development, claimed that class struggle in the countryside was not dead, warned of the restoration of capitalism, advocated that the production brigade be the basic accounting unit, and praised the Cultural Revolution "new born things."[9]

A common and often-repeated theme in these and other speeches during 1974 was the Criticize Lin Biao and Confucius Campaign (Pi-Lin, Pi-Kong). Every one of Zhao's speeches was laced with the rhetoric of this campaign. For example, in a speech to a meeting on "Strengthening Marxist Theorists" in July, Zhao said the following:

> At present, to continue to deepen the struggle to criticize Lin Biao and Confucius, further expose and investigate the conspiratorial activities in Guangdong of the Lin Biao antiparty clique, further criticize the true ultrarightist nature of Lin Biao's counterrevolutionary revisionist line, criticize the doctrine of Confucius and Mencius and the mentality of worshipping Confucius and opposing the Legalist school and make it penetrating, universal, persistent and systematic—all this demands that we read and study still better,

grasp the weapon of theory, and gradually build a mighty force of Marxist theorists in the course of struggle. Only in this way can we enhance still better our awareness of the line struggle, distinguish right from wrong in line, and carry the struggle to criticize Lin Biao and Confucius through to the end.[10]

This quotation is typical of the rhetorical quality of Zhao's speeches during this period. Whether he was addressing a conference on industry and communications, the PLA, propaganda work, or gymnastics, all successes were attributed to the proper understanding of this campaign, while all failures were attributed to not "grasping it properly."[11] As was the case with most campaigns, the latitude for local-level interpretation was quite broad. This campaign in particular had gone through several phases since its inception following the Tenth Party Congress, and it had fluctuated broadly in its purpose and content. Basically, the campaign vacillated back and forth between what Merle Goldman calls the "bureaucratic group" and the "Shanghai group."[12] Each group used it to attack the other, albeit in allegory.

Zhao's major role in the campaign was not the vitriolic rhetoric of his speeches, but rather some actions which were not readily apparent. In Zhao's new capacity as first Party secretary and chairman of the Revolutionary Committee (he had been promoted to both posts in April 1974), Zhao rehabilitated several former members of the Red Flag (Rebel) faction of Red Guards and appointed them to responsible positions in running the "Pi-Lin, Pi-Kong" campaign. For example, Mo Jingwei, the leader of the former 1 August Combat Corps, was appointed as vice director of the "Pi-Lin, Pi-Kong" staff office. This was an interesting turn of events because it was the Red Flag faction which had dominated the sheng ge lian alliance and had overthrown Tao Zhu and Zhao in 1967, while the East Wind (conservative) faction had supported and cooperated with Zhao.[13] Why should Zhao cooperate with those who had previously toppled him from power? The answer lies in the internecine factional strife within the sheng ge lian after it had come to power. The Red Flag faction had split apart in 1968 and three of the dissident leaders were arrested: Li Zhengtian, Chen Yiyang, and Wang Xizhe. These three individuals adopted the collective pseudonym Li Yizhe. Just before his arrest in August 1968, Li Zhengtian had written a wall poster protesting against the harsh suppression of Red Guards by the Huang Yongsheng-led Guangdong Military District Command. Likening this action to a fascist dictatorship, he vowed to continue the struggle. Upon his release from detention in 1971, after the Lin Biao affair, Li and his colleagues began to discuss and write about the dictatorial nature of Lin Biao and the need for socialist democracy and law. Together, "Li Yizhe" wrote an article containing their thoughts, signed it, dedicated it to "Chairman Mao and the Fourth National People's Congress" (expected shortly), and sent it to Beijing via special courier in December 1973.[14] The messenger was apprehended by the authorities en route to Beijing (but still in Guangdong), and the captured document was forwarded to Zhao Ziyang.[15] Zhao had the Li Yizhe article printed and made available for internal circulation (neibu faxing) among cadres within the province.[16] Their criticisms had struck a responsive chord with Zhao. They were not reprimanded but rather encouraged personally by Zhao and Guangdong Military Region commander Xu Shiyou to continue writing.

Li Yizhe's next article, titled "What is to be Done in Guangdong?," was written in April 1973 as a wall poster (dazibao). Despite the official ban on wall posters, issued in the form of Central Directive (zhongfa) No. 17, the poster was put up and allowed to stay up for two days. Zhao probably acquiesced to allowing the poster to stay up that long.[17] The poster claimed that there were still people in Guangdong who were preventing the masses from thoroughly criticizing Lin Biao. The poster sparked several others which all, in one way or another, criticized the "Lin Biao system." Realizing that this "poster war" could be of use in the campaign, Mao reversed himself and personally lifted the ban on posters in zhongfa No. 18 in May. Throughout the summer of 1974 wall posters appeared all over the country attacking local cadres for everything from having special privileges to obstructing the rehabilitation of Cultural Revolution victims. Li Zhengtian had become somewhat of a cause celebre. He was thought to have his finger on the pulse of the masses, and in fact Zhao and Xu Shiyou met with Li every Wednesday to listen to the "opinion of the masses."[18] Moreover, Zhao instructed Nanfang Ribao to appoint Li as an "investigator on social problems."[19] In his new job, Li set out to gather information on the crimes of Lin Biao and Huang Yongsheng in Guangdong; he discovered that about 40,000 people had been killed during the Cultural Revolution in the province.[20]

On 10 November "Li Yizhe's" most scathing poster was put up on Beijing Road in Guangzhou. Titled "On Socialist Democracy and the Legal System," the poster was an expanded version of the original 1973 article. It stretched for over 100 yards along the street and contained 20,000 characters. The poster's content was a sweeping indictment of the Cultural Revolution and those who led it. It listed six demands or "expectations" of the National People's Congress. First, laws should be enacted to protect the "democratic rights" of the masses. Second, steps should be taken to prevent the emergence of a privileged elite. Third, measures should be adopted to guarantee the right of the masses to supervise the leaders of the Party and government. Fourth, strict regulations should be adopted to prohibit torture, frameups, revenge and other forms of "fascist dictatorship." Fifth, government and Party policies should not fluctuate so often.

Sixth, the principle of "from each according to his ability, to each according to his work" should be adopted. This poster was too much for the center to tolerate. Li Xiannian and Ji Dengkui declared it a counter-revolutionary document, and Jiang Qing declared that it was "the most reactionary article yet since Liberation."[21] An opposing poster was quickly written under the aegis of the Guangdong CCP committee and was put up on 3 December. Thereafter, "Li Yizhe" was charged with various forms of sedition, and a "criticize Li movement" was launched throughout the province. The three members of "Li Yizhe" were separately criticized in various units throughout Guangzhou. Li Zhengtian was personally subjected to over one hundred criticism and struggle meetings, the largest of which involved 10,000 people at Zhongshan University in January 1975.[22] However, at these criticism sessions "Li Yizhe" were allowed to refute their critics' charges at length, thus airing views which Zhao and the provincial CCP Committee probably supported but which they could not publicly express.[23] Following these sessions, "Li Yizhe" disappeared and remained in detention until 1979 when they were released, and then rearrested after the closure of Democracy Wall. Their case also became a cause célèbre to many foreigners, including Amnesty International. In retrospect, "Li Yizhe" can be considered early forerunners of the 1979 Democracy Wall Movement.

The case of "Li Yizhe" illustrates that while Zhao was rhetorically promoting the "Pi-Lin, Pi-Kong" campaign wherever and whenever he could during 1973-1974, he used it to attack the "radicals" and their policies. The "Li Yizhe" movement bourgeoned in large part because Zhao permitted it. To be sure, there were also those at the center who desired it to continue and used it for their purposes (i.e., Zhou Enlai and Deng Xiaoping).

In early 1975, the "Criticize Lin Biao and Confucius" campaign died out and was replaced by the so-called "Dictatorship of the Proletariat" campaign. This campaign was initiated by the Shanghai "radicals," notably Yao Wenyuan and Zhang Chunqiao. Chairman Mao gave his support to the campaign in its early stages,[24] but he did not sustain his support as the radicals attempted to manipulate the campaign (as they had with "Pi-Lin, Pi-Kong") in their on-going battle with Zhou Enlai and Deng Xiaoping. Zhou and Deng had the political initiative after the January 1975 Fourth National Peoples Congress (where Zhao Ziyang was elected a member of the Presidium). At the Congress, Zhou made his famous speech calling for the attainment of the "Four Modernizations" (agriculture, industry, science and technology, and national defense) by the end of the century. Not only were the Four Modernizations set forth as the national goal, but also a series of pragmatic and programmatic policy documents were drafted under the supervision of Deng Xiaoping. With Zhou already suffering from cancer, Deng had been promoted at the Second Plenum of the Tenth Central Committee meeting (8-10 January 1975) to the posts of vice chairman of

Zhao Ziyang meeting with delegates to the Guangdong Poor and Lower Middle Peasants Association Conference, June 1965.

Zhao Ziyang chatting with peasants at a conference during the Socialist Education Movement in 1965.

After his 1971 rehabilitation from Cultural Revolution disgrace, Zhao Ziyang meets with peasants in Qingshuihe County, Inner Mongolia Autonomous Region.

Having returned to Guangdong and restored as first secretary of the Revolutionary Committee, Zhao Ziyang makes an investigation of the 1974 fall harvest.

Transferred to Sichuan Province in December 1975 as first secretary of the CCP Committee, Zhao Ziyang gives instructions for relief work in the aftermath of an earthquake in Pingwu County, Sichuan, August 1976.

Having turned Sichuan Province into an economic model for national emulation, Zhao Ziyang takes time off work to climb the famous Mount Emei, August 1979.

Having replaced Mao's heir Hua Guofeng as Premier of the State Council, Zhao Ziyang visits Beiling Park in Shenyang, Liaoning Province during September 1980.

An advocate of China's "open door" policy of trade with foreign countries, Zhao Ziyang inspects an imported Japanese rice thrasher in Jilin Province during an inspection tour in August 1980.

Zhao Ziyang talks with workers at the Daqing oil field in northeast China in February 1981.

Premier Zhao Ziyang sharing a laugh with Communist Party General Secretary Hu Yaobang at the Twelfth CCP Congress in September 1982.

the CCP, member of the Standing Committee of the Politburo, and Chief of Staff of the PLA. At the NPC, Deng was also made the leading vice premier.

The "radicals" had reason to worry. They therefore turned to the "Dictatorship of the Proletariat" campaign as the medium to launch their counterattack. Through a series of pseudonymous writing groups (e.g., Liang Xiao, Zhou Si, and Luo Siding), the radicals began to attack the modernization program put forth by Zhou and Deng as a means of restoring "bourgeois rights." They were particularly critical of the use of material incentives to increase productivity. They not only attacked the domestic implications of the modernization program, but also its international implications. By using historical allegory, these writing groups argued that the importation of technology from abroad was part and parcel of the "comprador" philosophy, which instead of augmenting China's security and independence did just the opposite.[25]

For his part, Zhao Ziyang was quick to endorse the campaign just as he had done with "Pi-Lin, Pi-Kong." On 2 March 1975 Zhao convened and addressed a provincial CCP Committee "report-back" meeting (huibao huiyi) on the campaign. Again the language Zhao used in his speech was uncharacteristically rhetorical and propagandistic; it closely paralleled the tone of the campaign at the center which was currently in its most "radical" phase. One week earlier Yao Wenyuan had published an article which attracted much attention (his first signed article in seven years), in which he warned of a "new bourgeoisie" arising within the Party. The means to counter this trend, Yao argued, were renewed class struggle, the "two line" struggle, and attacking "empiricism."[26] Upon examination, we can see that Zhao's speech paralleled Yao's very closely, e.g.:

> The class struggle in society will inevitably be reflected within the Party. While grasping well the class struggle in society through applying the weapon of the theory of the dictatorship of the proletariat, we must also grasp well the struggle between the two lines in the Party and promote the revolutionization of the leadership groups. The question of the struggle between the two lines in the leadership groups can only be seen more clearly through lifting the lid off the class struggle in society and only by solving the problems in the leadership groups, enhancing their line awareness and further revolutionizing them, can we grasp still more forcefully the struggle between the two classes and two roads in society. . . . In combining study with reality, we must also conduct social investigation and conduct research into the situation in the current class struggle and in policy, including economic policy. We must support the socialist newborn things, reduce and eliminate step by step the traces of the

old society and advance towards the lofty goal of communism. . . .
At present, we must primarily overcome empiricism and the ten-
dency to look down on theory and replace the study of theory with
grasping actual work. This point must be particularly emphasized
among the leading cadres at the county level and above.[27]

From this excerpt, it is clear that Zhao was paying very close attention to the campaign and its current leftist emphasis. Zhao clearly had
identified himself with Yao and the radical left. This speech, taken
together with Zhao's aforementioned speeches of 1974 and others he made
in 1975 (e.g., on art and literature, and industry),[28] indicates that following
his rehabilitation Zhao was much more careful to echo the more leftist
central policy line than he had been prior to the Cultural Revolution. Prior
to his purge, as we have previously seen, Zhao frequently contradicted
leftist policies with which he did not agree. Zhao's lexicon had also
changed; his formerly candid and objective analysis was replaced by rhetorical and subjective language. It can only be concluded that Zhao's
Cultural Revolution experience made him more "leftist" in the content of
his public speeches. I see this change on Zhao's part as more opportunistic
than real because of his long and well-documented association with "conservative" policies which, as we will see in the next section, he reasserts
with a vengeance.

NOTES

1. NCNA (Beijing), 22 May 1971.

2. Interview in Guangzhou, 23 May 1981. The exact location of
this school is unclear, but in July 1983 Zhao made an inspection tour of
Hulun Buir prefecture in Inner Mongolia. It is possible that Zhao was
returning to the place where he spent much of the Cultural Revolution
period, but this is, of course, conjecture. After the visit he published an
article praising the prefecture for implementing the household responsibility system (baogan daohu). See Zhao Ziyang, "Strengthen Unity, Do a
Good Job of Construction," (Zengqiang tuanjie, gaohao jianshe), Minzu
Tuanjie (National Unity), No. 8, August 1983, pp. 2-7.

3. Zhao's identification as "vice-chairman" on these occasions is
to be found, respectively, in: Renmin Ribao (hereafter RMRB), 15 May
1972; RMRB, 15 July 1972; RMRB, 16 August 1972; RMRB, 3 September
1972; RMRB, 24 November 1972; and RMRB, 16 October 1972.

4. For an account of the Lin Biao affair, albeit questionable in its
authenticity, see Yao Mingle, The Conspiracy and Death of Lin Biao (New
York, 1983).

5. See for example Jurgen Domes, China after the Cultural Revolution (Berkeley, 1977), ch. VI.

6. Stanley Rosen, Red Guard Factionalism and the Cultural Revolution in Guangzhou (Berkeley, 1982).

7. RMRB, 16 April 1973.

8. Foreign Broadcast Information Service Daily Report—People's Republic of China (hereafter FBIS), 26 June 1974, p. 1.

9. FBIS, 10 December 1974, pp. H1-11.

10. FBIS, 3 July 1974, pp. H3-5.

11. See, respectively, FBIS, 11 July 1974, pp. H5-7; FBIS, 27 September 1974, pp. H3-5; FBIS, 2 August 1974, pp. H3-5; and FBIS, 12 December 1974, pp. H2-4.

12. Merle Goldman, China's Intellectuals: Advise and Dissent (Cambridge, 1981), pp. 166-91.

13. Stanley Rosen, "The Democracy Movement in Guangzhou," paper delivered to the Association for Asian Studies Annual Meeting (2-4 April 1982), unpublished. I thank Professor Rosen for sharing with me his detailed analysis of Guangdong Red Guard factionalism. Much of the following analysis draws upon his research.

14. Ibid., p. 7.

15. Ibid.

16. Ibid.

17. I wish to thank Merle Goldman for bringing this point to my attention.

18. Rosen, "The Democracy Movement in Guangzhou," p. 10.

19. Ibid.

20. Ibid.

21. Ibid., p. 11.

22. Dong Xiang No. 5, 1979, cited in Chinese Law and Government (Summer 1981), p. 53.

23. Goldman, China's Intellectuals, p. 191, and Rosen, "The Democracy Movement," p. 16; both agree on this point.

24. In an article in the 9 February RMRB, Mao argued "Why did Lenin speak of exercising the dictatorship of the proletariat over the bourgeoisie? Bourgeois rights can only be restricted under the dictatorship of the proletariat." For a thorough discussion of this campaign, see Goldman, ibid., pp. 191-201.

25. See for example Liang Xiao, "The Yang Wu Movement and the Slavish Comprador Philosophy," Lishi Yanjiu, No. 5 (20 October 1975), translated in Survey Mainland China Magazines (hereafter SCMM), No. 7536 (16 December 1975), pp. 1-10. For a survey and analysis of the debates of this period relating to Chinese foreign policy, see Kenneth Lieberthal, "The Foreign Policy Debate in Peking as Seen Through Allegorical Articles, 1973-76," China Quarterly No. 71 (September 1977), pp. 528-54.

26. Yao Wenyuan, "On the Social Base of the Lin Biao Antiparty Clique," Beijing Review, No. 10 (7 March 1975).

27. FBIS, 7 March 1975, pp. H4-7.

28. For his speech on literature and art see FBIS, 26 July 1975, pp. H3-4; for industry see FBIS, 9 July 1975, pp. H1-3.

6
The "Sichuan Experience": Blueprint for a Nation, 1976–1979

In November 1975 Zhao was transferred to Sichuan Province, and one month later he was identified as first Party secretary.[1] In January 1976 he assumed the additional post of first political commissar of the Chengdu Military District. Zhao's transfer from Guangdong to Sichuan was not unique. Throughout 1975 Deng Xiaoping moved to restaff senior provincial positions with rehabilitated cadres. Zhao was one of nine such rehabilitees appointed as first secretaries, with countless more appointed at central, regional, and district levels.[2] Moreover, Sichuan was Deng's native province and he was said to have been very distressed over the backward economic and leftist political conditions there during an inspection trip in 1975.

What kind of situation did Zhao have to contend with when he arrived in Sichuan? What was the shape of the political and economic landscape? First of all, Sichuan is China's most populous province and is larger than many nations. At the time of Zhao's arrival its population was in the range of 80–90 million, of which over ninety percent resided in rural areas. This large population, the large territorial mass (approximately the size of France), and the endowment of natural resources was at the same time a burden and a source of strength to the Chinese national economy. Sichuan both drained and contributed to the nation's resources. Its reputation for being China's "rice bowl" was slipping. Food grain output was officially claimed to have reached record levels in 1974 (60–70 million jin), although only twenty-eight counties and municipalities had in fact reached or exceeded the grain output target of the annual plan.[3] This level of output was sufficient to feed the province, but it allowed for little export. This fact distressed central planners since Sichuan had long supplied deficient provinces with a variety of foodstuffs. Similarly, the Sichuan industrial sector was not producing as expected, although it too had registered impressive annual increases. Official statistics registered a 34 percent increase in the net value of industrial output between 1970 and 1974, with the largest increase coming in chemical fertilizer, natural gas, and sugar production.[4] Steel production, iron ore, and coal exploitation were lagging despite substantial deposits. Moreover, the communication and transport infrastructure was weak causing frequent bottlenecks in planning and delivery of materials, respectively. Thus in the economic realm, despite genuine qualitative and quantitative increases since 1949, the Sichuan economy remained basically stagnant and barely self-sufficient.[5] The political environment was not in much better shape. The Cultural Revolution strife had hit Sichuan hard,[6] and the provincial leadership was still putting its house in order when Zhao arrived. To be sure, Zhao's assignment to Sichuan was intended to stabilize the provincial polity and stimulate the economy.

Zhao's first appearance in Sichuan was on 19 December 1975 when he delivered a speech to work teams conducting propaganda in rural areas. He cited the need for on-site inspection teams, the rectification of leadership groups, the need to "learn from Dazhai," and "taking class struggle as the key link, we must persist in the Party's basic line, promoting agriculture, consolidating the dictatorship of the proletariat and developing the various fronts of the Great Proletarian Cultural Revolution and the movement to criticize Lin Biao and Confucius."[7] From this speech we can see that Zhao, the newcomer, was not going to leave a flank uncovered. He cited all of the fashionable slogans of the time. His penchant for this had carried over from his post-rehabilitation Guangdong speeches.

The year 1976 began with the death of Premier Zhou Enlai on 9 January and the ensuing attacks on Deng Xiaoping which culminated in his second downfall following the Tian'anmen incident in April. In February and March wall posters criticizing Deng arose in Sichuan which paralleled those in Beijing in both tone and timing.[8] In March Zhao too was criticized in wall posters in Guangzhou for being an "unrepentant right deviationist."[9] With the attacks on both Deng and himself, and being in a new environment, Zhao was in an increasingly vulnerable position. What did he do? As might be surmised from his past behavior in similar situations, Zhao adopted a "wait and see" strategy; he lay low, remained silent, and did not appear in public between 27 January and 8 April—two days after Deng's official ouster. The intervening forty-eight hours permitted Zhao to ascertain from the Central Committee documents that the purge was not likely to go any further than Deng, and that a compromise had been reached within the Politburo on appointing Hua Guofeng "first vice chairman" of the CCP and Premier of the State Council. Zhao broke his silence on 8 and 9 April when he spoke to a rally to "hail the two resolutions of the Central Committee" (dismissing Deng and appointing Hua to the aforementioned posts). At these meetings Zhao was identified in all of his positions as first CCP secretary, chairman of the Revolutionary Committee, and first political commissar of the Chengdu Military District. His position appeared intact. To make sure, at the 9 April rally, Zhao is quoted as calling on the army, Party, and people at all levels to "thoroughly expose and criticize the crimes of Deng Xiaoping who vainly attempted to subvert the dictatorship of the proletariat and restore capitalism" (emphasis added).[10]

The campaign to criticize Deng Xiaoping was on. Zhao had gone on record once and that was enough as far as he was concerned. As the campaign unfolded in the provincial newspapers (e.g., Sichuan Ribao)[11] and in the provincial Party Committee,[12] Zhao was nowhere to be seen or heard. He missed the May Day rally where provincial CCP secretary Duan Zhunyi criticized Deng (Duan took the lead in this task at other provincial rallies and conferences). Two weeks later Zhao appeared at two rallies (one on "tracking down counterrevolutionaries in the province" and another hailing the anniversary of the 16 May Circular), but he did not speak at either session.[13] Two weeks later Zhao played host to the touring Nepalese King Birendra for a week, and then disappeared from public view for more than two months during the summer. In late August he led an inspection team to an earthquake-striken area of northern Sichuan. On this occasion Radio Chengdu identified Zhao in all three of his major provincial posts as if to reassure the public that he had not fallen from power in Deng's wake.[14] We do not know whether or not Zhao came under fire within the Party during this period, but aside from the early wall posters there is no public evidence of attacks on Zhao which tied him to Deng either explicitly or implicitly. Judging by his behavior it appears that Zhao deemed his best chance to escape going down with Deng was to remain as invisible as possible, and therefore avoid having to publicly criticize Deng. Zhao did not criticize Deng to exploit the situation for his own gain as he could have (which many of his provincial colleagues did). By not doing so he demonstrated his loyalty to Deng. Further, Deng is known to have gone into internal exile in Guangdong under the protection of Guangdong Military Region commander Xu Shiyou and then first Party Secretary Wei Guoqing. Given Zhao's ties with these individuals and his long history in Guangdong, it is not beyond the realm of possibility that he too had a hand in this arrangement. Deng was not to forget Zhao's allegiance at this crucial juncture.

On 9 September Mao Zedong died. Zhao was appointed as a member of his funeral committee and flew to Beijing. A week later Zhao returned to Chengdu to preside over a memorial service for the late Great Helmsman. Unsure of the future course of events, Zhao played it safe by echoing the central line of the time in his eulogy:

We must resolutely <u>act according to the principles laid down</u> by Chairman Mao and the Central Committee. We must persist in <u>taking class struggle as the key link</u>, persist in the Party's basic line and in <u>continuing the revolution under the dictatorship of the proletariat, struggle against capitalist roaders in the Party, against class enemies, against revisionism, and against capitalism.</u> . . . At present, we must concentrate our firepower to <u>criticize Deng Xiaoping in depth</u>. We must unfold the struggle <u>personally launched by Chairman Mao to criticize Deng Xiaoping and counterattack the rightist wind to reverse verdicts</u> (emphases added).[15]

Again we see Zhao going on record against Deng and making notably pro-Gang of Four statements. However, the two anti-Deng statements are hardly the central themes of his speech, and in the context of the entire speech they appear almost as afterthoughts. As was frequently the case with his provincial speeches,[16] Zhao did not raise specific criticisms of Deng such as the "three poisonous weeds," the "three freedoms," the "four bigs," the "theory of black and white cats," etc.

On 6 October the Gang of Four (Jiang Qing, Zhang Chunqiao, Yao Wenyuan, and Wang Hongwen) were arrested in Beijing. The next day the Politburo reportedly held an enlarged session to brief provincial leaders (who were flown in) on the arrest.[17] Although there is no public record of those attending the meeting, Zhao's position warranted his probable attendance. If he did attend this meeting, he quickly returned to Sichuan because, on the morning of 9 October, Zhao and the Standing Committee of the Sichuan CCP Central Committee held a meeting to "fervently support" the arrest of the Gang and Hua Guofeng's ascension to CCP chairman and head of the Military Commission.[18] At a mass rally of 800,000 on 23 October in Chengdu, Zhao berated the Gang of Four at length while mentioning the need to continue to criticize Deng Xiaoping only once.[19] In the following weeks, Zhao delivered two more speeches which leveled specific charges against the Gang for their activities in Sichuan:

In a word, the Gang of Four is the general source of evil in Sichuan's confusion and unrest, and the arch-criminals of sabotaging revolution and production in Sichuan. . . . It was the Gang of Four who sabotaged the Great Cultural Revolution in our province, instigated "strike down everything" and stirred up an all-around civil war, causing a long and large-scale armed struggle in Sichuan which suffered serious losses.[20]

At a conference held by the central authorities this February, when the Gang of Four suddenly attacked, labeled, struck blows at and frantically put pressure on the provincial CCP committee behind the backs of Chairman Mao, Chairman Hua and the Central Committee, in June, July, and August, the Gang feverishly pressed from above while a few persons in the province pressed from below. . . . The Gang of Four sent material, issued instructions, conveyed information by telephone, sent secret letters, set up secret contact points, formed their own system, and went their own way.[21]

On the subject of how to deal with the followers of the Gang, Zhao said:

As for people who have committed mistakes, we must treat them discriminatingly. Most of them made mistakes and committed wrong-doings under the influence of the Gang of Four. Only a very small number of them followed the Gang in doing vicious things and they fell in deeply. We must allow the comrades who committed mistakes to correct them. Once they have corrected them, it is all right. We must not cling to their mistakes without forgetting, getting entangled in old historical records, and kill them with one blow.[22]

We must not act like the Gang of Four and strike people down once and for all. . . . Chairman Mao taught us to "cure the disease to save the patient". . . . With regard to those few persons in our province who fell in very deep, we must also advise them that their only way out is to thoroughly confess things, expose and correct their mistakes. It is useless to hide, deny or try to get away with them. There is no merit in resisting stubbornly. All exposure and criticism of the Gang of Four must be carried out under the centralized leadership of the Party committees. We must not establish ties or form fighting teams of any description.[23]

Judging from his words Zhao had little interest in unleashing a vindictive vendetta. Indeed, there is no evidence of arrests of Gang followers for a year. Following a rally to commemorate the first anniversary of Mao's death, Liu Xingyuan (commander of the PLA Chengdu Military Region) disappeared and was later identified as a follower of the Gang. Then in February 1978 the "three factional chieftains" of the Gang in Sichuan were arrested (Deng Xingquo, Huang Lian, and Zhou Jiayu).[24] Later that year, in June, it was announced that the Gang's two chief allies in Sichuan (Liu Jieting and Zhang Xiting) had been arrested and subjected to fifty-three mass criticism sessions.[25] They were charged with "persecuting to death" more than one hundred cadres during the Cultural Revolution, "beating to death" another two thousand, and injuring more than eight thousand others.[26] Further, they were accused of writing secret letters to Jiang Qing and Wang Hongwen in 1976 asking for their assistance in overthrowing Zhao Ziyang and Zhao Cangbi (then a Sichuan Party secretary and head of Sichuan public security, later to become national Minister of Public

Security), and also sent their personal representative to Beijing to lodge their complaints with Mao in March 1976.[27] Judging from the available evidence, therefore, a sweeping purge of Gang of Four followers in the province does not appear to have taken place. While the major allies of the Gang were arrested, Zhao's call for voluntary confessions appears to have been heeded in several locales.[28] For his part, Zhao made it through one of the most tumultuous years of political turmoil since the Cultural Revolution. Now Zhao was ready to turn his attention to his main task—reviving Sichuan's economy.

Zhao ended 1976 by attending the Second "Learn from Dazhai" Conference in Beijing. Upon returning to Sichuan, he addressed a "report back" meeting (huibao huiyi).[29] The Sichuan CCP Committee General Secretary Li Ziyuan gave the keynote speech in which he criticized "the remnants of capitalism in many parts of the province" and "Liu Shaoqi's policy of 'three freedoms and one contract.' "[30] Zhao criticized neither of these in his speech, but rather dwelled on Mao's speech "The Ten Great Relationships" (which had recently been reissued). His failure to mention Dazhai was conspicuous by its absence.

Following closely on the heels of the provincial "Learn from Dazhai in Agriculture" conference came the provincial "Learn from Daqing in Industry" conference. Zhao delivered the closing address, in which his principle theme was that industry should serve agriculture.[31] In particular, he stressed the development of the "five small" industries (wuxiao gongye): fuel and raw materials, chemical fertilizer and pesticides, steel, irrigation devices, and farm tools. In his speech Zhao had much praise for "our wise leader Chairman Hua," much criticism of the Gang of Four, and ended on the odd note of encouraging cadres to "follow whatever Mao said and whatever he decided" (the "two whatevers," which was later used as evidence to topple the "small Gang of Four"—Wang Dongxing, Wu De, Ji Dengkui, and Chen Xilian).

After this February conference, Zhao remained relatively inactive for six months. He put in token appearances where protocol demanded, doing one stint of manual labor, and spending most of late June-early July on a rural inspection tour in the Sichuan countryside. The available public evidence does not list Zhao as attending the Third Plenum of the Tenth Central Committee in Beijing in July, when Deng Xiaoping was officially restored to his former posts. He did travel to Beijing a month later, however, to attend the Eleventh CCP Congress—where he was elected an alternate member of the Politburo. Altogether Zhao remained in Beijing a month, two weeks past the closing of the Congress, thus affording ample opportunity to meet with Deng Xiaoping and other leaders.

Bolstered by his new appointment, he returned to Chengdu to preside over the aforementioned purge of Liu Xingyuan. Liu was replaced as

Chengdu Military Region commander by Wu Kehua, while Zhao himself took up the post of first political commissar—thus reconsolidating provincial Party control over the military.[32]

Zhao's public appearances during the autumn do not merit mention, except perhaps at a provincial conference "on diversified economy." This meeting is significant because it was indicative of things to come.

During the second half of 1977 Zhao began to set in motion agrarian reform policies which, in time, attracted national and international attention. Whether or not these policies were directed from the center (or to what degree) by Deng and his "brain trust" in the Academy of Social Sciences (Hu Qiaomu, Xue Muqiao, Sun Yefang, etc.) is conjecture. What is known is that Zhao and the provincial CCP committee adopted "Regulations on a Few Major Issues in Present Rural Economic Policy," i.e., the "Twelve Rules on Rural Areas."[33] These rules stipulated that peasants could engage in private plots, limited household sideline production, and "free" markets (thus resurrecting "sanzi"), advocated the implementation of the principle "paying each according to his work" (anlao fenpei), and stressed that peasant incomes should be raised as high as possible. The "Twelve Rules" further provided that all production teams in which the annual grain rations per person was less than 360 catties (217 kilograms) were not required to store public grain, so as to insure higher personal income. Instead, individual households were encouraged to store grain for their own consumption. Gradually, contracts for grain production output quotas were first fixed upon the household (baogan daohu) and later, in some locales, on the individual (lianchan daolao).[34] The quotas were fixed and monitored by the production team. As long as peasants met the assigned quota in the time specified, the surplus was theirs to eat and/or sell on the "free" market. Further, production teams were authorized to pay cash bonuses to those individuals or households which overfulfilled the target. The policy of "specialized contracts" (zhuanye chengbao), by which the team signed contracts with individuals to produce specific sideline items, was also introduced. The items are purchased from the individual at a set price (specified in the contract), resold by the collective at a higher price, and the profit is redistributed to its members. Because the team remains the basic accounting unit (BAC), all of these reforms are still considered socialist because they adhere to Zhao's dictum that "as long as collective ownership is not changed, all kinds of modes of production can be practiced without exploitation."[35]

These policies immediately paid off. By Zhao's own account in his year-end address to the Fifth Sichuan Provincial People's Congress:

total (1977) grain production registered a ten percent increase over last year and cash crop production also increased. The annual state plan for total industrial output value was fulfilled sixty-five days ahead of time, with increases by large margins registered in iron and steel, coal, natural gas, power generation, chemical fertilizer, and freight transportation. The output value of commune-run industries rose more than one hundred percent compared with last year. The pace of capital construction was generally faster. The annual state plan for financial revenue was also overfulfilled.[36]

Zhao went on to say that the Gang of Four's "bourgeois factional network in Sichuan has been fundamentally smashed. The persons and events connected with the Gang's schemes to usurp Party and state power have been investigated and largely verified."[37] This reference was a forewarning of the announcement six weeks later of the arrest of the "three factional chieftains." Zhao closed his work report with a call for continued criticism of the Gang as the "key link" for 1978. In brief, the format and substance of Zhao's speech very closely paralleled Hua Guofeng's work report to the Eleventh CCP Congress in August.[38]

While it is noteworthy that Zhao was a pacesetter for implementing these rural policies as early as the fall of 1977 (a full year before they came into vogue nationally), it is important to note that he was not the only one taking such initiative. Wan Li in Anhui was also experimenting with similar incentive policies at the same time.

Zhao was very busy in 1978. His public visibility and concomitant publicity increased dramatically. He continued to broaden his involvement in various issue areas. He gave major addresses on science, education, agriculture, industry, finance and trade policy. He attended national meetings in Beijing, hosted foreign dignitaries in Sichuan, and traveled abroad for the first time in his life (as far as is known). Zhao accompanied Hua Guofeng to Romania, Yugoslavia, and Iran. What he saw in these countries seemingly influenced his economic thinking greatly, because upon return he instituted significant reforms in enterprise management.

On the first day of the year Zhao published an article in Hongqi. This was his first publication since before the Cultural Revolution. Entitled "Raise Ourselves to an All-Out Effort to Speed Up Construction in Sichuan in Order to Make More Contributions to the State and People," Zhao's article called for turning Sichuan into a "strategic rear base." The thrust of the article dealt with production targets for the 1977-1985 period. Zhao claimed that:

by 1985, the average per-hectare grain output (in Sichuan) will reach 7.5 tons and total grain output will top 1977 by 55 percent. The average income of every commune member will be 80 percent higher than in 1977. Total industrial output value will be 2.8 times that of 1977 with big increases in petroleum, iron, steel, and coal. The province will become self-sufficient in light industrial products and have a more or less complete national defense industrial system.[39]

By announcing these extremely ambitious targets, and the 1978-1985 time frame itself, Zhao was giving a sneak preview of the content of Hua Guofeng's work report and "Outline of the Ten-Year Plan for the Development of the National Economy, 1976-1985" which were presented at the Second Plenum of the Eleventh Chinese Communist Party Central Committee (CCP-CC) in February 1978,[40] and adopted at the Fifth NPC in March 1978.[41] Zhao's article was the product of months of document drafting in preparation for a central Party work conference in early January which set the agenda for the Second Plenum. Ironically, the overly-ambitious targets presented by Hua were used in 1980-1981 as evidence to topple him from the premiership, only to be replaced by Zhao himself. The argument could be made that Deng framed Hua by having a speech drafted which was intentionally overly ambitious.

Before Zhao went to Beijing to attend these national meetings, he attended and addressed a provincial "Finance and Trade Conference on Learning from Daqing and Dazhai." His speech lacked policy substance and was laced with Daqing/Dazhai rhetoric.[42] Also before leaving for Beijing he did manual labor at the Chengdu railway station, getting his photo on the front page of Sichuan Ribao.[43] More importantly, Zhao was visited by Deng Xiaoping from 31 January-3 February, when Deng stopped over in Chengdu between official state visits to Burma and Nepal.[44] Deng could have laid over in a number of other places, or could have gone directly from Burma to Nepal. The reasons for Deng's layover are only speculative, but one cannot help but sense that the two held a strategy session concerning Zhao's reforms and career.

In late February, Zhao went to Beijing to attend the aforementioned national meetings. He was elected, along with Deng, executive chairman of the Presidium of the Fifth National Committee of the Chinese People's Political Consultative Congress (CPPCC). The CPPCC is a body which had been defunct since the 1950s, but was revived in 1977 as an attempt to enlist the support of non-CCP members and overseas Chinese for Deng's modernization plan and "united front" policies for reunifying Taiwan and Hong Kong with the Mainland. At the ensuing NPC Hua Guofeng announced his grandiose economic development plans. Hua's work report and "Outline Plan" are examples par excellence of a "scissors and paste" speech, i.e., a few sentences or paragraphs are devoted to every special interest group.[45] Hua even went against his collectivist instincts and put his stamp of approval on Zhao's agrarian reform policies, noting the "constitutional right" of peasants to work private plots and engage in sideline production. Hua also proclaimed the investigation of associates of the Gang of Four "fundamentally concluded." Perhaps sensing that the purges of Cultural Revolution beneficiaries (like himself) were substantially reducing his political allies in the provinces and at the center, Hua felt the need to cut his losses. His attempts were to continue in vain for another year.

Perhaps spurred by Hua's call for 85 percent agricultural mechanization by 1985, upon his return to Sichuan Zhao convened and addressed a provincial agricultural mechanization conference. Perhaps sensing that Hua's goal was unrealistic and/or that assistance (i.e., machinery) from outside Sichuan was not going to be forthcoming, Zhao invoked the principle of "self-reliance" (zili gengsheng). "We can find no way out if we wait for, rely on, or demand assistance. Establishing a system of industries to support agriculture and bringing about agricultural mechanization depend on our hard work."[46]

Zhao is not listed as having attended either the National Science Conference in March or the National Education Conference in April in Beijing. Rather, he waited until July to convene provincial science and education conferences to which he delivered major addresses. He did, however, note the importance of the national science conference by speaking to a rally of lower-level cadres on the importance of the meeting, sponsoring a computer technology lecture series, and attending a provincial science and technology lecture.[47]

In May Zhao addressed a provincial work conference on "Learning from Daqing in Industry." He proclaimed the "movement to criticize one thing and rectify two" to be the central task of the year. The "one criticism and two rectifications" movement was to criticize the Gang of Four and rectify leadership bodies and enterprises. The "one criticism and first rectification" had been in full swing in the province since the Gang's downfall,[48] but the second rectification (aimed at enterprises) would not be implemented until the following fall after Zhao's return from Yugoslavia. Nonetheless, Zhao gave an insight into his thinking about the latter by saying:

> In straightening out the enterprises under the Party committee's leadership, we should implement the system of division of responsibility for factory managers and the systems of responsibility for chief engineer, chief account, and so on. We should establish a system of the workers congress or assembly, worker participation in management, cadre participation in labor, combination of leading cadres, workers and technicians, and other basic systems.[49]

It should be noted that the antecedents of these ideas can be found in Deng's 1975 "Some Problems in Accelerating Industrial Development" (later to be branded one of the "three poisonous weeds"). Furthermore, the timing of these remarks is significant because it shows Zhao going on record publicly before leading individuals at the center. For example, it was not until July when Hu Qiaomu (in an address to the State Council) called for management reform.[50]

On 1 July Zhao delivered the closing address to the Sichuan Education Conference. Unlike Deng's or Education Minister Liu Xiyao's addresses to the National Education Conference in April, Zhao did not discuss specifics of educational reform; this he left to his deputy Du Xinyuan. Rather, Zhao spoke generally about the economic and political situation in the province.[51] While at variance with Deng's speech on some specific points, Zhao's speech did parallel Deng's in spirit. He berated the "whatever faction" for not "seeking truth from facts" under the "new historical conditions." He spoke at length about the need for Party secretaries to become involved in day-to-day educational affairs, thus echoing Liu's speech but contradicting Deng. Like Deng, he cited the importance of key-point (zhongdian) schools.[52] Unlike Deng, he neglected to mention the red/expert cleavage, examination system, Young Pioneers or Communist Youth League (CYL), teachers, or down-to-the-countryside youth program (xiaxiang).[53]

Three weeks later Zhao delivered one of his most important (and lengthy) speeches during his tenure in Sichuan to the provincial Science Conference. Unlike his Education Conference speech, Zhao discussed specific subjects of needed scientific inquiry and experiment within the fields of agriculture, industry, mining, electronics, and animal husbandry. He spoke at length about the need for basic research, the "five-sixths principle,"[54] and reform of research institutes and their personnel. Both the tone and the substance of Zhao's speech was a synthesis of Deng's, Hua's and Fang Yi's speeches to the National Science Conference.[55] He took up some of the specific projects mentioned by Fang Yi. His discussion of treatment of scientists and researchers, science curriculum in education, ties to the international scientific community, etc., paralleled Deng's speech very closely. In a significant break with Deng's idea of training an elite corps of scientists, Zhao implored: "We must acquire full understanding of Chairman Hua's strategic thought of raising the scientific and cultural level of the entire Chinese nation . . . and arming the broad masses with up-to-date scientific knowledge" (emphases added).[56] Thus, in this speech, we see Zhao selectively drawing upon other leaders' speeches so as not to leave himself open to criticism from any quarter.

One week later Zhao returned to Beijing to begin background briefings for his trip with Hua to Romania, Yugoslavia, and Iran. Just prior to departure military leader Luo Ruiqing passed away; Zhao was on the funeral committee and attended the memorial service. On 14 August, the entourage departed for Bucharest. Zhao was listed third in rank order behind Hua Guofeng and Ji Dengkui. This was Zhao's first known trip abroad.

The delegation spent five days in Romania. Aside from the symbolic value of visiting the Soviet's "backyard," there was nothing particularly noteworthy about the itinerary. Zhao participated in all of Hua's activities, including the talks with President Ceausescu. One can speculate that one subject of these talks was Sino-American relations. Ceausescu had visited Washington in April, just a few weeks before the Brzezinski trip to Beijing in May which initiated the negotiations for normalization of relations. The United States had used Ceausescu previously as an intermediary to carry messages to Beijing.[57] While being a member of the Warsaw Treaty Organization (WTO), Ceausescu had managed to distance Romania from the Soviet Union and practiced a versatile foreign policy.

From Romania, the delegation traveled to Yugoslavia. Again, Zhao was present at all of Hua's activities, and he also participated in working-group discussions with Ji Dengkui and their Yugoslav counterparts. One subject of these discussions and Hua's talks with Tito was the Yugoslav experience in economic enterprise management. For example, in the 27 August talks: "President Tito briefed Chairman Hua Guofeng and his associates in detail on the economic achievements in Yugoslavia. He placed particular emphasis on the period of decentralization and of the development of self-management from its introduction in 1950 until the present."[58] In addition to the activities mandated by protocol, the delegation visited several model factories and a dairy farm, pointing up the special interest the delegation had in the economic policies of Yugoslavia. The third leg of the trip was a three-day visit to Iran. Zhao attended talks with the Shah and other leaders. The delegation returned to China from Tehran.

Why was Zhao, a provincial official, included on this important delegation abroad? Again, we lack hard evidence, but can offer educated conjecture. First, Deng was grooming Zhao for a high-level government position and wanted to increase his exposure to affairs of state. Zhao had never been abroad, did not know how high-level discussions with foreign leaders were conducted, and had minimal knowledge of the specifics of various contemporary international problems. All three of these deficiencies could be somewhat alleviated by participating in the trip. Second, with the delegation headed by Hua Guofeng and Ji Dengkui, neither of whom Deng could consider political allies, he (Deng) "planted" Zhao in the delegation so as to and report back to him on the talks. This is a tactic frequently employed by leaders involved in factional disputes, as Deng and Hua were at that time. Third, Deng and his economic advisors at the Chinese Academy of Social Sciences (CASS) felt that Yugoslavia and Romania had much to offer China in the area of economic reform, particularly in enterprise management. The Chinese press, and particularly the special economics journals, had since early 1977 been publishing a variety of articles on Romanian, Yugoslavian, and to a lesser degree other Eastern European economies. These articles primarily focused on infrastructural and technological issues, while not addressing issues of management reform. This changed dramatically after the delegation's return.[59] What Zhao saw and heard must have impressed him because shortly after his return to Sichuan he instituted significant reforms in enterprise management. Before turning to the content and scope of these reforms, which constitute the most important aspect of Zhao's activities during the second half of 1978, Zhao's other activities during this period will briefly be described.

First, it is important to note that the economic success of Sichuan, and Zhao personally, began to receive increased national publicity beginning in late summer. Zhao was praised in Beijing in August for resolutely moving against Gang of Four followers, carrying out cadre rectification and consolidation of "leading bodies," and personally "reversing the verdicts" on two previously framed cadres.[60] The effects of the agricultural reforms, and Zhao's role in them, were given frequent detailed attention in the national press, for example,

> While political stability was being restored, leading cadres on the provincial Party committee went to the countryside to investigate and work out methods for a quick recovery of the rural economy. The peasants especially appreciated the efforts of Zhao Ziyang. He visited scores of counties, sometimes going directly to the fields to work alongside the peasants and acquire first-hand knowledge of what the peasants demanded of the provincial authorities. Two years ago, peasants in many localities were forced by provincial decree to grow two rice crops plus one crop of wheat or rape annually. This arbitrary way of doing things caused disaster because Sichuan had neither enough money or fertilizer nor machines for growing three crops a year. Zhao Ziyang and others proposed and the provincial Party committee adopted a decision for 1977 first to restore the traditional double-cropping system of wheat-rice, and second to cut the total triple-cropping hectarage by 266,000 hectares. The total output of rice increased by 1.2 million tons over 1976.[61]

In November the New China News Agency (Xinhuashe) published a five-part series on rural reforms in Sichuan which appeared in a number of newspapers and journals nationwide.[62]

Second, Zhao's appearances for the September-December period include:

— hosting foreign delegations from Nepal, North Korea, and Romania;

— attending memorial services for deceased (and in the case of Peng Dehuai and Tao Zhu posthumously rehabilitated) comrades;

— leading a provincial delegation on an inspection tour of Jiangsu;

— speaking to provincial meetings on agriculture, on the "criterion for truth," and nationality affairs.[63]

Thus we see Zhao keeping a high profile, speaking out on a wide range of issues, and taking part in a wide range of activities. Significantly, however, Zhao is not reported as having attended the extremely important Third Plenum of the Eleventh Central Committee held in Beijing from 18–22 December (despite his status as an alternate member of the Politburo), although he did appear in Beijing two days later with other state leaders for a memorial service commemorating Peng Dehuai and Tao Zhu. The only Politburo members reported attending the Third Plenum were Chen Yun, Deng Xiaoping, Deng Yingzhao, Hu Yaobang, Hua Guofeng, Li Xiannian, Wang Dongxing, Wang Zhen, and Ye Jianying.

Zhao's most significant endeavor during this period, though, was in industrial enterprise reform. Agricultural enterprise reform (i.e., commune and brigade-run sideline production), which had been in vogue for the better part of a year, was already proving its worth. So Zhao turned his attention to industry. Convinced that economic planning was too highly centralized, Zhao likened the existing industrial management structure to a silkworm wrapped in a cocoon.[64] As long as the state dictates production plans by fiat, allocates all raw materials, capital equipment and manpower, purchases and markets all products, takes all profits, and protects the jobs of all workers, then inefficiency, bottlenecks, and poor product quality are to be expected. Zhao was quick to embrace the then-heretical views put forth by Hu Qiaomu (president of CASS), in a speech to the State Council in July.[65] The most significant aspects of Hu's speech dealt with management reform—mixing market mechanisms with planning, expanding the decision-making powers of enterprises, developing "specialized companies" (zhuanye gongsi), and learning the management practices of other countries, including capitalist nations. Having thus "liberated his thinking" (jiefang sixiang) and receiving the stamp of approval from the center, Zhao proceeded to direct the expansion of the decision-making power in various enterprises to increase production.

In October 1978, six industrial enterprises in Sichuan were granted expanded autonomy on an experimental basis.[66] These experimental enterprises were granted the "eight rights":[67]

(1) Right to retain part of the profits. The profits kept by the enterprise can be used to pay bonuses to workers, improve auxiliary facilities for workers, or be channeled back into production.

(2) Right to expand production with funds accumulated by the enterprise.

(3) Right to retain 60 percent of the depreciation fund for fixed assets, as against 40 percent in the past.

(4) Right to engage in production outside the state plan, only after the state plan has been met.

(5) Right to market their own products which the commercial or materials departments do not purchase.

(6) Right to contract with foreign governments to export their products and to reserve part of the foreign exchange earnings for the import of new technology, raw and other materials, and equipment.

(7) Right to issue bonuses at the enterprise's own discretion within the broad guidelines approved by the state.

(8) Right to penalize those who incur heavy losses to the state due to negligence in work or other subjective reasons.

These enterprises proved successful in increasing output and raising the income of member workers. The number of experimental enterprises quickly multiplied to 100 by the end of 1978 and to 417 by the end of 1979. In early 1979 Yunnan and Anhui provinces began similar experiments under the tutelage of two other Deng proteges—An Pingsheng and Wan Li respectively—and by July the State Council granted approval to increase the number to 4,000 nationwide.[68] By the end of 1980 the national total had reached 6,000.[69]

Needless to say, a number of facets of these policies are anathema to the Maoist legacy, e.g., the seeking of profits and using them as a criterion of enterprise viability, issuing of cash bonuses, firing workers, and lifting price ceilings to respond to demand. But, at the same time, it is important to point out that worker participation in management was a consistent Maoist hallmark. The difference between Mao's and Zhao's perspectives on this subject are a matter of degree, of the proper mix. That is, the two dimensions of participative management—worker participation in management and managerial control—may be conceptually independent, but are not mutually exclusive in practice. It is not a zero-sum relationship. An increase in worker participation does not necessarily imply a decrease in managerial control, and vice versa.[70]

In another significant borrowing from the Yugoslav experience, Zhao instituted a policy of "consolidating enterprises." In so doing, Zhao concentrated on the creating of horizontal links between different types of production units: state-owned factories, state farms, commune and brigade enterprises, urban cooperatives, and scientific research institutes on a joint investment basis.[71] This policy of enterprise integration took five forms:[72]

(1)   the incorporation of a large enterprise "based on the ownership of the whole people" with a small local enterprise into a joint investment venture;

(2)   the incorporation of an enterprise "based on the ownership of the whole people" with an enterprise based on collective ownership into a joint investment venture;

(3)   the joint investment and operation of two enterprises in the production of a certain commodity;

(4)   an enterprise jointly invested in and run by a leading urban industrial unit or an enterprise "based on the ownership of the whole people," and a commune or production brigade; and

(5)   the joint operation by a scientific research unit and a factory.

Zhao ordered the establishment of enterprises which combined agriculture, industry and commerce. For example, twenty-six state farms on the outskirts of Chongqing were amalgamated into the Yangzi Agriculture-Industry-Commerce Joint Enterprise.[73] This particular project was so successful its claimed profits totalled 1.7 million yuan in 1979, as compared with 40,000 yuan in 1978, and annual deficits before 1977.[74] As a result, similar joint enterprises were set up in more than thirty Sichuan counties and municipalities by July 1980.[75] By practicing this integrated system, factories purchased raw materials directly from communes and brigades, and sold their goods directly to stores or external buyers without the involvement of local government.[76]

To be sure, these reforms were not without problems. Zhao himself reportedly admitted:

Since the broadening of the decision-making power of enterprises, funds at their disposal have been used quite irregularly; the percentage of profits that various factories keep have been different; and with the readjustment of the marketing mechanism, various enterprises have blindly rushed to produce the same commodities that would bring high profits, thereby causing unbalanced production and waste.[77]

One might add to Zhao's list of unanticipated problems the fact that individual enterprises negotiating with foreign firms, without central coordination from Beijing, caused an overextension of contracts--which were sharply curtailed by the center in 1980-1981. It is only natural to expect problems when introducing new policies of such a sweeping nature. Hence further refinement of policies and methods of implementation were needed. The extended period of "readjustment" (tiaozheng) is meant not only to alleviate bottlenecks and imbalances left over from the past, but also some caused by these new policies.[78]

During 1979 Zhao continued many of his activities and policies begun in 1978. His public visibility remained high. He became involved in an increasing range of issues (trade unions, women's issues, birth control, forestry, sports, youth affairs, militia work, foreign policy), thus strengthening himself as a political generalist—a necessary credential for high national office. His main policy bailiwick continued to be economic reform, and he became increasingly interested in questions of economic theory. He again traveled abroad, this time leading a provincial delegation to Great Britain, Switzerland, and France. He played host to visiting dignitaries from West Germany, Nepal, the Netherlands, Britain, and Yugoslavia. Zhao also spent a good deal of time traveling the country to lay wreaths and/or participate in memorial services for deceased comrades, many of whom had been previously rehabilitated. He attended no fewer than thirteen such functions for twenty-four individuals, many of whom Zhao had known or worked with in Guangdong before the Cultural Revolution.

Zhao's first major activity of the year was to deliver probably his most important speech during his entire tenure in Sichuan. Coming on the heels of the important Third Plenum of the Eleventh Central Committee (18-22 December 1978), which was a watershed event in the post-Mao era, Zhao addressed the Third Sichuan CCP Congress in Chengdu. In order to put Zhao's speech in perspective, let us review the conclusions of the Third Plenum. The plenum, dominated by Deng Xiaoping, decided:

- to conclude the mass movement to criticize Lin Biao and the Gang of Four;
- to shift the Party's work for 1979 to socialist modernization;
- to lay stress on agricultural production;
- to cancel the "erroneous" documents concerning the 1976 "Tian'anmen incident";
- to "reverse the erroneous verdicts" on Peng Dehuai, Tao Zhu, Bo Yibo, Yang Shangkun, and others;

— to elect new members to the Central Committee, Politburo, and create a Central Commission for Inspecting Inter-Party Discipline; and

— to reevaluate Mao Zedong's achievements and theories.[79]

Concomitant with shifting the Party's focus to modernization, the thrust of the Plenum dealt with economic issues. It put its stamp of approval on many of Zhao's reforms, to wit:

> The session points out that one of the serious shortcomings of the structure of economic management in our country is the over-concentration of authority, and it is necessary to boldly shift it under guidance from the leadership to lower levels so that the local authorities and industrial and agricultural enterprises will have greater power of decision in management under the guidance of unified state planning; big efforts should be made to simplify bodies at various levels charged with economic administration and transfer most of their functions to such enterprises as specialized companies or complexes; it is necessary to act firmly in line with economic law, attach importance to the role of the law of value, consciously combine ideological and political work with economic methods and give full play to the enthusiasm of cadres and workers for production; it is necessary, under the centralized leadership of the Party, to tackle conscientiously the failure to make a distinction between the Party, the government and the enterprise and to put a stop to the substitution of government for enterprise administration, to institute a division of responsibilities among different levels, types of work and individuals, increase the authority and responsibility of administrative bodies and mangerial personnel, reduce the number of meetings and amount of paperwork to raise work efficiency, and conscientiously adopt the practices of examination, reward and punishment, promotion and demotion. These measures will bring into full play the initiative, enthusiasm and creativeness of four levels, the central departments, the local authorities, the enter-prises and workers, and invigorate all branches and links of the socialist economy.[80]

Zhao's speech echoed these themes, paralleled others from the plenum, and went further in a number of areas.[81] The bulk of his work report dealt with economics. He made a numer of specific proposals to stimulate output in agriculture, industry, the defense industries, mining, animal husbandry, etc. On the subject of enterprise reform, Zhao had this to say:

The main contents of the reform areas follows: . . . allow the enterprises in particular more right to independent action; under a unified state plan, planned economy should be integrated with market economy; the practice of determining sale according to production should gradually be switched to determining production according to demand; apply the law of value and bring into play the role of economic devices such as pricing, credit, and taxation. We must implement the principle of distribution according to work and material incentives so as to get the enterprises and workers concerned with the enterprises' performance, profit, and accumulation in light of their own material interest. Streamline the administrative structure and set up various specialized companies and complexes. Cut down on administrative intervention and allow the different economic setups to play their role. . . . We must resolutely move ahead with reform projects that are readily effective and within our reach. First, expand the power of the enterprise to allow it a certain limited right of independent action in regard to manpower, financial and material resources, supply, production and sale. Second, expand the scope of giving awards and piece-rate wages, reinstate and improve certain single item prizes. Third, with the approval of higher authorities, the enterprise has the right to sell its own products and new items not purchased by the departments of commerce, material goods, and supply and marketing. Fourth, establish enterprise funds in every business unit and the employees congress has the right to decide on the use of the funds. Fifth, institute the system of employees' congress and employees' general assembly, which will exercise the right of democratic management; cadres at the workshop and production team levels are to be chosen by the masses through a democratic election.[82]

Zhao's speech also touched on a number of other matters, many of which we have seen in his previous speeches, and they fall in the following categories: science and technology (almost word-for-word of his Science Conference speech), foreign trade, democracy, the Gang of Four and their followers, exonerated cadres, separation of Party and government, regulations for inter-party conduct, and the effects of the "rightist-phobia" ossifying the thinking of cadres (i.e., refusing to implement the new reforms for fear of being branded a "right deviationist").[83]

Zhao's other activities during the first quarter of 1979 include:

— addressing an enlarged Standing Committee meeting of the Sichuan CCP-CC on the economic tasks for 1979-1982. In this talk, Zhao not only addressed economic projects and policies, but also class struggle. He made three points: "(1) Class struggle is not an end, but a means to liberate productive forces. After the completion of socialist transformation of the means of production, there is still class struggle, but it becomes less and less acute. (2) To wage class struggle is not our aim, but rather to emancipate the productive forces. (3) What class struggle remains belongs to 'contradictions among the people' (not between the people and the enemy), and should therefore be handled accordingly."[84] This speech had a strong ideological focus.

— attending and addressing a panel discussion of Chengdu economic theorists. The panel discussed how to combine a market economy with a planned economy, improving product quality, management reform, agricultural mechanization, banking, and how to strengthen the study of economic theory. Concerning the latter, it was concluded that the Sichuan Academy of Social Sciences should hold twice-weekly discussions of economic theory, step up efforts to acquire theoretical materials from abroad, and begin a magazine. Further, province-wide meetings should follow any national meeting on economic theory.[85]

— attending and addressing another forum of economic theorists. The agenda and conclusions of the meeting are almost identical to the previous one.[86] This meeting was preceded the day before by a conference on the Yugoslav and Japanese economies where representatives of the Institute of Economics of CASS lectured.[87] Three days later, Zhao attended another forum on "the law of prices," with representatives from other provinces and national departments under the State Council and CASS.[88] This appears to have been a week-long series of meetings jointly sponsored by various Sichuan bureaus and institutes and attended by leading economists from Beijing and other provinces.

— attending the Sixth Sichuan Trade Union Congress.[89]

— attending the Fifth Sichuan Women's Congress.[90]

— attending the Sixth Sichuan Communist Youth League Congress.[91]

— attending the Fourth Sichuan Provincial Sports Meeting.[92]

— planting trees in Chengdu.[93]

During this period, Zhao also attended a number of memorial services for posthumously rehabilitated cadres, including his former mentor Tao Zhu. Tao Zhu died of cancer of the pancreas on 30 November 1969 while incarcerated in Hefei, Anhui province.[94] According to his daughter, Tao Zhu had languished in prison in Beijing after his downfall in 1967 until mid–October 1969 when Lin Biao's Order Number 1 had him (and Liu Shaoqi) moved out of the capital. Just prior to this move, Zhou Enlai had personally arranged for surgery to be performed, but it was too late. Tao was a dying man.[95] In memory of Tao Zhu, Zhao published an article in the People's Daily entitled "The Noble Quality of Communists." This article is very revealing about what Zhao thinks of his former mentor. The entire article is worth reading, but the following passages are illustrative:

> I worked directly under Comrade Tao Zhu for fifteen years. The impressions he gave me are deeply imprinted on my mind. I will never forget him as long as I live. . . . He was resourceful, a man of decision and great perseverance, full of vigor and vitality. He worked selflessly, untiringly, very efficiently and was highly creative. . . . He did everything and charted work policies and seldom confined himself to hard and fast rules. He was observant and had a quick mind. He was good at grasping principal contradictions in a complicated situation and boldly opened up new situations. We comrades who worked under him felt Comrade Tao Zhu was always superior in tackling a task and approaching a problem. . . . He had a strong will. It was not easy to make him change his mind once he decided upon a problem. He was quick-witted and learned rapidly. He was also quick to respond to questions. In discussing a problem he often interrupted others and aired his views. Those who did not know him well thought that he was overly confident and could hardly accept other people's opinions. After getting along with him for some time, they would find that he treated others as equals in discussing a problem. One of his important features was that he was sharp, pungent and vigorous, never discussed a problem in vague terms, but said yes for yes and no for no and dared to air his views. . . . Sometimes he would argue heatedly with you and might even be unhappy with you. Yet he never bore this in mind. He boldly used comrades around and under him, readily shouldering responsibility for their mistakes and never shifting the blame to others. . . . Full of vigor and vitality, he did his work very concretely. He never took a day off. As soon as he would discover a problem, he would assign someone to solve it. . . . He worked selflessly for the public interest, led a simple life and never regarded himself as someone special. When he went to the countryside on an inspection trip, he always took a minimum retinue with a jeep or station wagon. He opposed extravagance and showing off. He forebade the local cadres to hold greetings or send–off parties and feasts in his honor or to give him gifts. . . . He never advocated the mountaintop–stronghold mentality and sectarianism.

He knew his subordinates well and appointed them according to his merits. . . . Some comrades said that Comrade Tao Zhu inherited the ancient Chinese statesmen's style of "respecting one's subordinates" and "thirsting for talented people." They were right. . . . In particular, he was good at uniting with intellectuals. Among his friends were men of letters, scientists, artists, professors, overseas Chinese, and generals who had revolted and come over. . . Demand less of others and give others more; unhesitatingly lay down one's life and go through thick and thin for the people's interests. This is what Comrade Tao Zhu said to the Chinese youth, exhorting them and pinning his hopes on them. This also was the Marxism with which he exhorted himself and which he did his utmost to achieve. Throughout his glorious life he strictly adhered to this criterion.[96]

Zhao's visible support of exonerated high cadres (like Tao Zhu), intellectuals and artists is only symptomatic of the rehabilitations taking place in Sichuan itself during Zhao's tenure. Between the downfall of the Gang of Four in October 1976 and December 1978, 4,600 individuals were said to have been rehabilitated.[97] By March 1979, however, signs of foot-dragging were prevalent enough to warrant a strongly-worded Sichuan Ribao editorial titled "Continue To Do Well in Promoting the Work of Reinvestigating and Correcting Unjust, Trumped-up and Incorrect Cases.[98] This procrastination may be viewed as part of a nationwide counterattack on the Dengist policies of the Third Plenum. In March/April a number of articles appeared in the central and regional press criticizing the new economic and foreign trade policies, problems associated with the February-March 1979 Vietnam incursion, the strengthening of relations with the West (notably the normalization of relations with the United States), the liberal policies on dissent (Democracy Wall) and the arts, etc.[99] The PRC-affiliated Hong Kong press dubbed this the "April Adverse Current." Beginning in mid-April, Deng's supporters began a counterattack of their own in the regional press.[100] Zhao reportedly joined this movement by publishing a strongly worded article in the national press criticizing the "April Cold Wind" and defending the line of the Third Plenum.[101] These efforts worked. By May the criticism died down and eventually the "small Gang of Four" (Ji Dengkui, Chen Xilian, Wu De, and Wang Dongxing) were purged at the Fifth Plenum of the Eleventh CC in February 1980. This group had been the locus of intra-leadership opposition to Deng and his policies after the purge of the Gang of Four.

As part of the effort to popularize Third Plenum policies and counter the "April Adverse Current," the Sichuan reforms received increased attention in the national media during the spring.[102] For its part, the Sichuan regional press began to publicize its own accomplishments with vigor. During the month of June, for example, hardly a day passed without <u>Sichuan Ribao</u> carrying a lead story or featured editorial on economic reform in the province.[103] One provincial story that the national press was eager to get out was the abolition of thirty-four "leadership groups, their offices and temporary offices" in an effort to cut bureaucratic waste and duplication of function.[104] Some three hundred cadres lost their jobs as a result. This streamlining was described as follows:[105]

> Before the Cultural Revolution, Sichuan had seventy-three provincial-level Party and government organizations. After the Cultural Revolution, nine were simplified and merged into other organizations. However, eighteen new organizations were set up. As a result, the total number of cadres involved increased from over 8,700 to over 11,000. The organizations abolished at this time belonged to both Party and government departments. Because the Party committee handles the work of government departments and because there is no division between Party and government, organizations overlap. . . . As a result, two systems appear to oversee the same work. Departments having political powers and functions receive leadership mainly from Party committee departments, but, at the same time, also receive leadership directly from offices of all government departments, thus creating an intricate and complex system. Many comrades believe that if, under the Party committee's unified leadership, we let departments having specific functions and powers under the political power system take charge of specific work in production and construction and curtail the immediate organizations, efficiency can be improved.[106]

This was the first move toward the separation of Party and government functions. The opposition to Deng's Third Plenum policies was serious enough for Zhao to devote a keynote speech to the Second Plenum of the Third Sichuan CCP Congress to the subjects. Zhao said:

> To carry forward the spirit of the Third Plenum, it is necessary to overcome the interference by two erroneous trends of thought within the Party and in society. One of the two trends is that a few comrades within the Party, who still don't want to liberate their minds (<u>jiefang sixiang</u>), have failed to correctly understand the spirit of the Third Plenum. . . . The other erroneous trend of thought in society is one that doubts and opposes the "four upholds"—the upholding of the socialist road, the dictatorship of the proletariat, the Party leadership and Marxism-Leninism-Mao Zedong Thought. This is doubting and opposing the third plenary session from the right side. It was not that these two trends of thought came into being

after the third session, but they did surface in early post-session days. Both trends run counter to the policy of the third plenary session. . . . It will take a fairly long time and great effort to solve these questions. Questions of petrification and semi-petrification of the mind still exist in the Party. The problem of being obsessed with lingering fear has yet to be solved as far as a considerable number of comrades are concerned. . . . Because the pernicious influence of Lin Biao and the "gang of four" has not yet been completely eliminated, some comrades have doubts about the correctness of the principles and policies adopted by the central authorities. Third, they waver when a gust of wind blows. They even consider the principles adopted by the third plenary session to be "rightist" or "deviationist." This view is entirely wrong and very harmful. . . . In the past, Sichuan was seriously affected by factionalism. In the struggle to expose and criticize the "gang of four," the general situation has been good but it cannot be said that the question of factionalism has been completely solved. In some areas and units, factionalism is still active, though not so openly, interfering with the implementation of Party policies and principles and is affecting the Party's unity. In strengthening Party building, we must be determined to solve the question of factionalism well. Of course, we do not have to launch a movement. We should mainly conduct ideological education and draw a line of distinction between right and wrong.[107]

Perhaps another rectification movement was not necessary, but Zhao and the provincial Party committee took steps to curb inner-Party dissent by establishing a special Committee for Inspecting Party Discipline, which first met in early June 1979.[108] This action paralleled the decision taken at the Third Plenum to establish a similar committee at the center under the direction of Chen Yun.

Following the Second Plenum of the Third Sichuan CCP Congress it was announced that Zhao would lead a provincial delegation to Western Europe during the month of June. By so doing, Zhao missed the Second Session of the Fifth National Committee of the CPPCC and the Second Session of the Fifth NPC, which were convened in Beijing during mid-month. Deng Xiaoping presided over the CPPCC, Ye Jianying over the NPC, and Hua Guofeng gave an important work report to the latter.

The first stop on the trip was England. In London Zhao and his entourage met with the Sino-British Trade Council and second-echelon officials in the government's Office of the Environment, Office of Foreign and Commonwealth Affairs, Office of Agriculture, Fisheries and Food, and the Institute for Agricultural Engineering, and members of Parliament.

Their week-long itinerary was diverse but dominated by agricultural activities. They visited various farms in the midlands, an agricultural fair, Bedford Agricultural College, and food processing factories. From Britain the delegation flew to Switzerland. During their four days there "the delegation visited with great interest a number of agricultural, industrial, and tourist facilities and exchanged views and experiences on questions of common interest with Swiss government officials and friends."[109] From Geneva the delegation traveled to Paris where Zhao met with the Foreign Minister, the Minister of the Interior, President of the National Assembly, President of the Senate, and Minister of Foreign Trade. Zhao's interlocutors in Paris were of higher rank than in London. After leaving Paris, agriculture dominated the itinerary. During their ten days in France the delegation toured the regions of Haute Normadie in the north and Languedoc-Rousillon in the south. They visited the port of Le Havre, agricultural establishments and cooperatives, food industries and other factories, and agricultural research centers such as the famous L'Ecole Nationale Superieure D'Agronomie in Montpellier.[110] From Paris the delegation flew home.

Zhao next appeared in public one month later in Chengdu to address a provincial conference on farmland capital construction. Zhao delivered an "important speech" to this meeting, the text of which is unavailable. The conference, however, dealt with the issues of improving yields, alleviating drought, afforestation, water conservancy, erosion and soil improvement, hydroelectric and natural gas sources.[111]

In late August Zhao hosted Nepalese King Birendra and in mid-September Dutch Prime Minister Uyl, both in Chengdu. Other than these three brief appearances, the public record reveals nothing about Zhao's activities during the summer. He very possibly could have been in Beijing preparing for his ascent, six months later, to the premiership.

Zhao next appeared at the Fourth Plenum of the Eleventh CCP-CC in Beijing (25-28 September). He took another important step towards national power by being elected a full member of the Politburo.[112] Zhao also reportedly had an important hand in drafting the document "Decisions of the Central Committee of the Communist Party of China on Some Questions Concerning the Acceleration of Agricultural Development," which was adopted at the plenum.[113] This document confirmed many of the agricultural reforms Zhao had already implemented in Sichuan, including:

— The right of ownership by the people's communes, production teams and their power of decision must be protected effectively by law and no unit or individual is permitted to deprive them of or encroach on their interests.

— While adhering to the socialist orientation, implementing the policies, laws and decrees of the state and following the guidelines of state plans, <u>all basic accounting units</u> of the people's communes <u>have the right to grow what is suited to local conditions, to decide on measures for increasing production and methods of management, to distribute their own products and money</u> and to resist arbitrary decision from any leading organ or person.

— No unit or individual is permitted to commandeer manpower, land, livestock, machinery, funds, products and material resources from people's communes, production brigades and teams apart from what is provided for in the state plan.

— Government departments are not permitted to increase the expenditure of the collectives and commune members when setting up enterprises and undertakings in the countryside apart from what is stipulated in state laws and decrees.

— It is essential to keep to the principles of <u>voluntary participation</u> and mutual benefit in building agricultural improvement projects and developing commune enterprises.

— Economic organizations at various levels of the people's communes must conscientiously implement the principle of "<u>from each according to his ability, to each according to his work</u>," and shall give more pay for more work, no pay to anyone who does not work, and equal pay for equal work irrespective of sex. It is imperative to work out payment in accordance with the amount and quality of work done, to establish the necessary system of reward and punishment and <u>firmly overcome egalitarianism</u>.

— Small plots of land and animals for private use by commune members, domestic sideline occupations, and village fairs ("free markets") are adjuncts of the socialist economy, and must not be repudiated as capitalist factors.

— It is essential for the people's communes to stabily <u>continue the system of three levels of ownership with the production team as the basic accounting unit</u>. Where conditions are not yet ripe, and most of the members are against it, it is not permissable to change the basic accounting unit from the production team to the production brigade (key phrases are underlined for emphasis).[114]

Given what we have witnessed of Zhao's agricultural reforms in Sichuan and language used in his provincial speeches, his role in drafting this document is unmistakable. To be sure, he did not draft it alone. Wan Li's similar reforms in Anhui and his important March 1978 article in Hongqi suggest that his influence on the document was also great. It is this document which approved and stipulated the provisions of the nationwide implementation of the agricultural "responsibility system" (zirenzhi).

While in Beijing Zhao attended the National Day celebrations commemorating the thirtieth anniversary of the PRC. It is unclear how long Zhao remained in the capital after national day. He did not appear publicly until mid-November when he hosted (in Sichuan) two foreigners whom he had met on his two trips abroad: Sir John Keswick of the Sino-British Trade Council and Milka Planinc of the Central Committee of the Yugoslav League of Communists. In the interim Zhao missed appearing at two meetings--one provincial and one central--which he would normally attend: a conference of the Chengdu PLA General Political Department (GPD), and a CPPCC-sponsored Congress of National Democratic Parties.[115] Zhao ought to have attended the first by virtue of his position as First Political Commissar of the Chengdu Military Region, and the latter by being vice-chairman of the National Committee of the CPPCC (all of the other vice-chairmen were in attendance). Where was Zhao during this period? It is a good possibility that he remained in Beijing to prepare for his new responsibilities on the State Council. This would have been an opportune time to do so since Hua Guofeng, the man he would replace, was on a state visit to Western Europe. Further, after hosting the aforementioned foreigners in Chengdu in mid-November he again appeared in Beijing on the twenty-eighth and in Guangzhou on 12 December, both times for memorial services. Thus Zhao was again absent from Sichuan for a one-month period.

Zhao did appear on 25 December to deliver a joint-session closing address to the Fifth Sichuan Provincial People's Congress and the Fourth Sichuan CPPCC Committee. Although he did address these meetings it is odd that he neither presided nor gave the main work report. This he left to his subordinates Du Xinyuan and Lu Dadong, respectively. In many ways Zhao's closing speech had the ring of a farewell address (he would only remain in Sichuan for two more months). In it he struck the familiar themes: production teams' right of self-determination, enterprises' right of self-management, decentralization of decision-making, the need for intellectuals and technical experts, implementing the spirit and policies of the Third Plenum, and the economic progress made in the province during his tenure.[116] To be sure, much progress was made during this period. According to official Chinese statistics, between 1976 and the end of 1979 total value of provincial output rose by 61 percent, of which the agricultural sector increased by 58 percent and the industrial sector by 64 percent.[117] This is impressive if one only measures on the basis of output--which, as we have seen, is the litmus test of policy success for Zhao.

However, as in the case with most Chinese economic statistics, no base line figure is given, thus percentage increase figures are nebulous.

As in 1978, Zhao began the New Year by publishing a lengthy article in the first issue of Hongqi. This afforded Zhao a good opportunity to stake out his policy positions in a national forum before ascending to national office. Entitled "Study the New Situation and Fully Implement the Principle of Readjustment,"[118] Zhao's article was divided into four sections: industry, agriculture, commerce, and readjustment. With regard to industry, he advocated expanding the self-management rights of three hundred experimental enterprises in Sichuan, making production responsive to market demand, increasing the supply of raw materials for production, and energy conservation. In agriculture, Zhao contradicted Fourth Plenum decisions on agricultural mechanization by speaking against it and advocating "the scientific method" of agriculture:

> The greatest efficiency of mechanization is that it saves manpower; it does not necessarily increase output very much. In particular, in places with a large population and little farmland, it does not play an especially great role in increasing production. Therefore, judging by present conditions, it is not an urgent task to promote very great efforts to promoting mechanization. In agricultural modernization, we must therefore lay stress on studying the application of modern science and technology in agriculture. Sichuan is already grasping this work. We have much to do in promoting the scientific feeding of animals and scientific crop cultivation. In short, we must now stress science. . . . Apart from that, we must continue to carry out agricultural capital construction in a measured way. I am not talking about farmland capital construction here, but about agricultural capital construction. . . . The farmland capital construction we once talked about was in certain respects narrow in content. We only mentioned water conservancy, land and soil improvement. This was too limited. The scope of agricultural capital construction is somewhat more extensive. It includes water conservancy and soil improvement, but also includes the construction of animal mating centers, seed stations, grain drying grounds, and warehouses. . . . Why are there so many tractors on the road and so few in the fields? Obviously, transport work can only be carried out away from the fields.[119]

With regard to commerce, Zhao wrote of the problems in procurement and marketing, and advocated "reviving the methods of 1957." Lastly, Zhao wrote of readjustment:

The questions I have mentioned above all come under the general heading of the three years of readjustment. . . . In the past the crux of the contradiction in economic work was too long on the capital construction front with too much investment. This squeezed aside agriculture, light industry, and people's living standards. The key to readjustment is to reduce accumulation, cut capital construction and strengthen the weak links. . . . However, readjustment is certainly not only a matter of cutting capital construction. It is a profound reform touching on all fields.[120]

From this we can see that Zhao was in step with current policies, and had adopted much of economic planner Chen Yun's thinking.

A few days after his Hongqi article appeared, Guangming Ribao carried an article reporting a recent meeting that Zhao had with "responsible persons of some institutions of higher learning in Sichuan."[121] True to form, Zhao advocated increased autonomy to institutions of higher learning. He put forth a proposal, which was adopted by the provincial Party committee, which stipulated the following:

After fulfilling the planned tasks in the stipulated teaching, scientific research, and laboratory works, the school may control the income in the following ten areas: the income from production contracts with external units and from sales of products in the school's practice and experimental factories; income from contracts and outside units in conducting experiments, calculation, chemical analysis, translation, designing, specimen-making, drawing and printing; income from the transfer of results of scientific research and from doing scientific trials for outside units; income from sales of products from scientific research; income from tuitions and fees of short-term training classes not included in the plans, of advanced students, after-work universities, and correspondence classes; a portion of the income of teachers, administrative personnel, and workers from participating in (extra) paying jobs that have to be handed over to the state; royalties from manuscripts and performances; income from lectures and publications, experimental farms, experimental forests, husbandry, horticulture; income from service charges to outside units in the use of halls, reception rooms, and vehicles. . . . As the proportion of distribution in the use of school funds of the institutions of higher learning, the concerned departments should make suitable decisions on the basis of giving priority to increasing the income of the individual administrative personnel and the workers. The school has the authority to take out one-third or one-half of the total amount from the income of the school funds to be used as bonuses to be distributed to the administrative personnel and the workers according to this decision. Bonuses given out to personnel in teaching and scientific research should be slightly higher than that to administrative personnel and workers. Those groups or individuals who have made great contributions can also be given year-end bonuses. The rest can be used in supplementing and updating teaching, scientific experimental equipment, and in improving the school conditions and the collective welfare measures of the teachers, students, and workers.[122]

During January and February Zhao only put in token appearances at tea parties, a PLA rally, and a memorial service. His term in Sichuan was finished. He appeared in Beijing throughout March and in April was identified (by Deng Xiaoping in an interview with Japanese journalists) as running the day-to-day work of the State Council.[123] In September 1980, at the Fifth NPC, Zhao was confirmed as Premier of the State Council, replacing Hua Guofeng. In Sichuan, Zhao left his subordinates Lu Dadong and Du Xinyuan in charge. Another aide, Du Xingyuan, accompanied Zhao to Beijing to assume the important post of secretary-general of the State Council. Zhao was succeeded as first Party secretary by Tan Qilong, who had held the same position in Qinghai province. As of mid-1983 Tan Qilong has been replaced, Lu Dadong has retired, Du Xinyuan is chairman of the Sichuan People's Congress, and Du Xingyuan was relieved of his duties in June 1983 and has not been reported in a new position.

What was Zhao's legacy in Sichuan? Clearly Zhao's primary impact was in the economic sphere. The policies he carried out collectively became known as the "Sichuan experience," which all of China was directed to study and emulate. These policies include:

— the "eight rights of enterprises";
— the reintroduction of the "three freedoms and one contract" system;
— the approval of profit-seeking as an economic goal and measure of enterprise viability;
— the integration of economic units as in Yugoslavia;
— the coexistence of planned and market economies;
— the establishment of a material incentive bonus system;
— the system of payment based upon work done;
— the adoption of more rational management techniques;
— the revival of of those with technical expertise;
— the willingness to seek help from abroad;
— the reform of academic curricula and research priorities;
— the stress on science and technology;

— the separation of Party and government; and

— the subordination of military to civilian rule.

The latter four are not economic policies per se, but certainly impact upon economic management and production. Birth control also affects the economy. During Zhao's tenure in Sichuan, China's most populous province, the population growth rate was the lowest in the country (0.67 percent).[124] In August 1979 Sichuan was dubbed as a national model to emulate, and Zhao was publicly given credit for turning the province around on the birth control front.[125]

Indeed, Zhao turned the province around on a number of fronts. Despite natural calamities, in the course of four years (1976–1979) Sichuan went from being a grain-importing province to an exporting one, regaining its title as "China's rice bowl." Aggregate grain output for this period increased by approximately 25 percent, growing from 24,850,000 million metric tons (mmt) in 1976 to 32,060,000 mmt in 1979. Per capita grain output similarly increased, growing from 260 to 328 kilograms.[126] Per capita annual grain consumption increased from 184 to 261 kilograms over the same period.[127]

Zhao was able to reap political capital from these economic gains. It not only earned him the respect of higher authorities, but also the populace. This is perhaps best captured in an eight-character Chinese phrase (chengyu) which was popular in Sichuan at the time: "If you want to eat, look for Zhao Ziyang" (Ni yao chiliang, kan Zhao Ziyang). The point is also that many of the policies Zhao pursued in Sichuan became national policy. The "Sichuan Experience" became a model for national emulation, central documents were based on earlier enactments in Sichuan, and Zhao himself became Premier. Zhao's rise was not entirely of his own doing, however. The strong and consistent patronage of Deng Xiaoping during the 1970s was a decisive factor in Zhao's rise to the top. Several of Zhao's policies emanated from Deng and advisors at CASS. They helped set the broad policy framework within which Zhao formulated and implemented specific measures. Nor could he have undertaken his initiatives without support or approval from the center. During his tenure in Sichuan we have seen Zhao employ three tactics with regard to central policy. Sometimes Zhao took initiatives and developed policies independently to suit local conditions, with the center publicly approving after the fact. Most of the time, however, Zhao followed the center's lead and implemented or advocated national policy directives. Other times, Zhao waffled by simultaneously echoing contradictory themes of a variety of central leaders. These three tactics illustrate how a provincial leader survives in the Chinese system.

To be sure, Zhao's and Deng's policies are not easily demarcated. Obviously they agree on much. But to give either Deng or Zhao all the credit for the "Sichuan Experience" flaunts the facts. Formulating the policies was at a minimum a joint effort. Being a conduit between central and provincial administration, and overseeing policy implementation were clearly Zhao's jobs. Those who actually implemented these policies at the local level, and those on the receiving end, must not be disregarded. To overlook them ignores much of what has been learned about the policy process in China over the last thirty years and takes us back to the simplified "totalitarian model" which holds that when Beijing commands, provincial officials obey, usually out of threat of coercion. What we have learned in the thirty odd years of the People's Republic, and especially since foreign social scientists have had opportunities to conduct field research on various aspects of policy implementation, is that spatial variance and bureaucratic inertia have placed the locus of responsibility for policy implementation at the local level. Therefore neither Deng Xiaoping, Zhao Ziyang, or the CASS economic planners can be individually credited with the success of the "Sichuan Experience." It was a collective effort.

NOTES

1. Interestingly, Zhao replaced Liu Xingyuan. Liu had risen to power in Guangdong during the Cultural Revolution and had been closely allied with Huang Yongsheng. Zhao had also replaced Liu in Guangdong in 1972. Thereafter, Liu was transferred to Sichuan and in February 1973 was named first Party secretary and first political commissar of the Chengdu Military Region. When Zhao arrived, Liu lost his Party post but was appointed commander of the Chengdu Military District. Liu held this position until 1977 when he was purged as an accomplice of Lin Biao and the Gang of Four. Zhao's reemergence on the political scene after the Cultural Revolution had twice come at the expense of Liu Xingyuan. The question further arises, however, of who Liu's patron was after the purge of Huang Yongsheng? Why did he not disappear sooner, along with the rest of Lin Biao accomplices? Further, who arranged for his transfer to Sichuan? Although there is no conclusive evidence, Zhang Chunqiao is a likely candidate because of his important role in personnel management during this period.

2. See Galen Fox, Campaigning for Power in China: 1967-76 (Ph.D. dissertation, Princeton University, 1979), pp. 221, 293; Earl A. Wayne, "The Politics of Restaffing China's Provinces," Contemporary China (Spring 1978), pp. 116-65; Parris Chang, Power and Policy in China (University Park, 2d ed., 1978), pp. 215, 307; Central Intelligence Agency Reference Aid, Appearances and Activities of Leading Personalities of the People's Republic of China, 1975 (Washington, D.C., 1975), p. 3.

3. Sichuan Radio, 16 August 1974, as cited in David S. G. Goodman, "Sichuan," unpublished manuscript. I wish to thank Professor Goodman for sharing with me this provincial study, which spans the period 1949-1975. Much of the background material on Sichuan in this section draws upon Professor Goodman's research.

4. Sichuan Radio, ibid., as cited in Goodman, ibid., p. 107.

5. A more gloomy assessment of Sichuan's agricultural and industrial condition in 1975-1976 can be found in Qian Taigang, "Zhao Ziyang's Critical Biography, Part III (1975-80)," (Zhao Ziyang Pingzhuan), Dang Dai (Hong Kong), 15 March 1981, p. 32. This source, which has proven to be quite accurate on mainland Chinese affairs in general and Zhao's career in particular, claimed that in 1975 and 1976 Sichuan was struck with such severe famine that neighboring Hubei province had to send grain into Sichuan for disaster relief. Moreover, this article claims that industry was depressed, consumer goods were in short supply, peasants were selling their children outside of the province, and all neighboring provinces were infiltrated with beggars from Sichuan.

6. See for example Thomas J. Matthews, "The Cultural Revolution in Sichuan," in Ezra Vogel (Ed.), The Cultural Revolution in the Provinces (Cambridge, 1971).

7. Chengdu, Sichuan Provincial Service (hereafter CSPS), 19 December 1975; Foreign Broadcast Information Service (hereafter FBIS, 23 December 1975), p. J1.

8. See for example CSPS, 9 April 1976, FBIS (14 April 1976), p. J4. Posters criticizing Deng began in Beijing in February; for a description of these, see David Zweig, "The Bei Da Debate on Education and the Fall of Deng Xiaoping," China Quarterly No. 73 (March 1978), pp. 140-59.

9. See for example Hong Kong Agence France Press (hereafter AFP), 1 and 17 March 1976; Paris AFP, 29 March 1976. These reports cite Guangzhou wall posters viewed on 28 February, 17 and 29 March 1976.

10. CSPS, 9 April 1976, FBIS (14 April 1976), p. J4.

11. See for example the Sichuan Ribao (hereafter SCRB) 12 April editorial "Seize the Opportune Time to Push the Struggle to Repulse the Right Deviationist Wind to Reverse Verdicts to a New Upsurge."

12. See for example two provincial CCP Committee telephone conferences to coordinate attacks against Deng: CSPS, 8 May 1976, FBIS (10 May 1976), p. J1; CSPS, 10 May 1976, FBIS (18 May 1976), p. J2.

13. CSPS, 11 May 1976, FBIS (12 May 1976), p. J1-2; CSPS, 17 May 1976, FBIS (19 May 1976), pp. J1-3.

14. Radio Chengdu, 19 August 1976, cited in Central Intelligence Agency Reference Aid, Appearances and Activities of Leading Personalities in the People's Republic of China, 1976 (Washington, D.C., 1976), p. 65.

15. CSPS, 18 September 1976, FBIS (20 September 1976), p. J3.

16. See for example "Sichuan Provincial CCP Telephone Conference on Political and Rural Work," CSPS, 7 October 1976, FBIS (8 October 1976), p. J1.

17. Chang, Power and Policy, p. 228 (Chang cites no source for this meeting); Andre Onate, in his article on the arrest of the Gang, also claims that there was a meeting, but says nothing of provincial leaders attending. See Andre Onate, "Hua Guofeng and the Arrest of the Gang of Four," China Quarterly No. 75 (September 1978), pp. 540-65.

18. CSPS, 11 October 1976, FBIS (13 October 1976), p. J3.

19. CSPS, 23 October 1976, FBIS (29 October 1976), pp. J5-8.

20. CSPS, 22 November 1976, FBIS (23 November 1976), p. J5.

21. CSPS, 4 December 1976, FBIS (8 December 1976), pp. J4-5.

22. CSPS, 22 November 1976. FBIS (23 November 1976), p. J6.

23. CSPS, 4 December 1976, FBIS (8 December 1976), p. J6.

24. CSPS, 12 February 1978, FBIS (15 February 1978), pp. J1-3. This report did not name who the "three factional chieftains" were. It was only in Zhao's speech to the Sichuan science conference in July 1978 that they were identified. The original text of Zhao's science conference speech is in SCRB (28 July 1978), and it is translated in David Shambaugh (Ed.), "Zhao Ziyang's 'Sichuan Experience': Blueprint for a Nation," Chinese Law and Government, Vol. XV, No. 1 (Spring 1982), pp. 35-69.

25. Beijing Xinhua Domestic Service (hereafter XHDS), 14 July 1978, FBIS (17 July 1978), pp. J1-3.

26. Ibid.

27. Qian Taigang, "Zhao Ziyang's Critical Biography."

28. See for example, "Prefecture in Sichuan Transforms Gang Followers," Beijing XHDS, 21 May 1978, FBIS (30 May 1978), pp. J1-2.

29. For a description of the role of these meetings in the policy process, see Kenneth Liberthal, Central Documents and Politburo Politics in China (Ann Arbor, 1978), pp. 29-30.

30. SCRB, 5 January 1977, p. 1.

31. SCRB, 14 February 1977, p. 1.

32. When Zhao arrived in Sichuan in 1975, the regional PLA forces (especially Chengdu city units) politically affiliated with the Gang of Four were strongly entrenched. For example, the 1976 anti-Deng campaign was vigorously pursued in these units, as is evident in CSPS dispatches of the time. The post-Lin Biao Incident reassertion of Party control over provincial/regional PLA units was uneven. Some MR commanders remained stronger vis-à-vis their civilian counterparts in the worker-peasant-soldier (gong-nong-bing) revolutionary committees than others; Chengdu Military District was one such case. For a more general discussion of this phenomenon, see my "The Role of People's Liberation in Chinese Politics," in Spring-Autumn Papers, Vol. III, No. 1 (Ann Arbor, 1981).

33. See for example, Qian Taigang, "Zhao Ziyang's Critical Biography."

34. For a discussion of the nationwide evolution of production quota contracts and the "responsibility system" (shengchan zirenzhi), see David Zweig, "Context and Content in Policy Implementation: Household Contracts in China, 1977-1983," unpublished paper presented to the workshop on Studies in Policy Implementation in the Post-Mao Era, Ohio State University, June 1983.

35. Qian Taigang, "Zhao Ziyang's Critical Biography."

36. Beijing XHDS, 1 January 1978, FBIS (19 January 1978), p. E24; for a full translated text see Shambaugh (Ed.), "Zhao Ziyang's 'Sichuan Experience,' " pp. 14-34.

37. FBIS, ibid., p. J5.

38. See Hua Guofeng, "Political Report to the Eleventh National Congress of the Communist Party of China," Beijing Review, No. 35 (26 August 1977), pp. 23-57.

39. Beijing XHDS, 19 January 1978, FBIS (19 January 1978), p. E24; for a full translated text see Shambaugh (Ed.), "Zhao Ziyang's 'Sichuan Experience,' " pp. 14-34.

40. For the text of the Plenum Communique, see Beijing Review, No. 9 (3 March 1978), pp. 7-8.

41. For the texts of Hua's work report and "Outline Plan," see Beijing Review, No. 10 (10 March 1978). For analysis of the Fifth NPC, see China News Analysis, No. 114 (24 March 1978), and FBIS Special Report on Communist Media, "The Fifth National People's Congress," No. FB 78-10005 (17 March 1978).

42. CSPS, 18 January 1978, FBIS (23 January 1978), pp. J1-3; SCRB editorial, FBIS, ibid., pp. J5-6.

43. SCRB, 7 February 1978, p. 1.

44. SCRB, 1 February 1978, p. 1 (front page photo of Deng and Zhao in embrace).

45. For an analysis of these documents, see FBIS Special Report on Communist Media, "The Fifth National People's Congress."

46. CSPS, 31 March 1978, FBIS (3 April 1978), p. J1. For text of the speech see SCRB (30 March). The bulk of Zhao's speech dealt with the backward nature of the "agriculture-support industries," poor management, the need for technical personnel, and the principle of "each according to his work."

47. These appearances are reported, respectively, in: CSPS, 16 April 1978 and FBIS (19 April 1978), p. J1; Beijing XHDS, 3 May 1978 and FBIS (8 May 1978), p. J1; and National Foreign Assessment Center, Appearances and Activities of Leading Chinese Officials During 1978, Vol. III, CR 79-12264, May 1979, p. 969.

48. On consolidation of leading bodies, see for example Beijing XHDS, 23 April 1978, FBIS (25 April 1978), pp. J2-3.

49. SCRB, 18 May 1978, p. 3.

50. For the texts of Hu's speeches see Beijing Review, Nos. 45, 46, 47 (10, 17 and 24 November 1978).

51. For translated excerpts of Zhao's speech see CSPS, 6 July 1978, FBIS (10 July 1978), pp. J1-3; the full text is in SCRB, 7 July 1978, and is translated in Shambaugh (Ed.), "Zhao Ziyang's 'Sichuan Experience,' " pp. 70-78.

52. Since March 1978 Sichuan had been running key-point schools on an experimental basis as directed by the Ministry of Education. See for example CSPS, 3 March 1978, FBIS (9 March 1978), pp. J6-7.

53. For the text of Deng's speech see Beijing XHDS, 25 April 1978, FBIS (26 April 1978), pp. E1-7.

54. The "five-sixths principle" was coined by Deng in his address to the National Science Conference. He said that scientists should spend at least five-sixths of their time in the laboratory, with little (or presumably no) time in political study. See FBIS (21 March 1978), p. E10.

55. Deng's and Hua's speeches differ markedly in tone and substance upon close reading. For the text of Deng's speech see Beijing XHDS, 21 March 1978, FBIS (21 March 1978), pp. E4-15. For the text of Hua's speech see Beijing XHDS, 25 March 1978, FBIS (27 March 1978), pp. E1-9. For the text of Fang Yi's speech see Chinese Science and Technology (Summer 1979), pp. 8-44.

56. Excerpts of Zhao's speech are in FBIS (10 July 1978), pp. J1-3; FBIS (24 July 1978), pp. J1-3; and FBIS (31 July 1978), pp. J3-6. The full text is in SCRB, 28 July 1978, and is translated in Shambaugh (Ed.), "Zhao Ziyang's 'Sichuan Experience,' " pp. 35-69.

57. See for example, Michel Oksenberg, "A Decade of Sino-American Relations," Foreign Affairs (Fall 1982), p. 176; Seymour Hersh, The Price of Power: Kissinger in the Nixon White House (New York, 1983), pp. 356, 359, 361, 365-66, 448-49.

58. Belgrade Tanjug Domestic Service (27 August 1978), FBIS-Eastern Europe (28 August 1978), p. I9.

59. I wish to thank Nina Halpern for bringing this to my attention and sharpening my sense of timing of these reforms. For a survey and analysis of these articles, see Nina Halpern, "Learning from Abroad: Chinese Views of the East European Economic Experience, 1977-1981," unpublished manuscript.

60. "Zhao Ziyang Implements Cadre Policy in Sichuan," Beijing XHDS, 6 August 1978, FBIS (8 August 1978), pp. J2-3.

61. "Sichuan's Rural Economy Recovers From Sabotage," Beijing XHDS, 27 September 1978, FBIS (28 September 1978), pp. J1-3.

62. Translations of parts 1-5 can be found respectively in FBIS (9 November 1978), pp. J2-3; Joint Publications Research Service (hereafter JPRS, 10 November 1978), p. 72; ibid. (11 November 1978), p. 68; FBIS (13 November 1978), pp. J1-2; JPRS (13 November 1978), p. 70.

63. For Zhao's appearances at the provincial meeting on agriculture, see CSPS, 8 October 1978, FBIS (12 October 1978), pp. J1-4; for meetings on "criterion for truth," see CSPS, 12 October 1978, FBIS (16 October 1978), pp. J1-2; and for nationality affairs, see CSPS, 30 October 1978, FBIS (2 November 1978), p. J1.

64. "The Sichuan Experiment With Enterprises," Beijing Review, No. 14, 6 April 1981, p. 21.

65. Hu Qiaomu, "Observe Economic Laws, Speed Up the Four Modernizations," Beijing Review, Nos. 45, 46, 47 (1978).

66. Beijing Review, No. 14, 6 April 1981, p. 23.

67. Ibid., p. 24.

68. Ibid, p. 23.

69. Ibid.

70. Andrew G. Walder, "Worker Participation in Enterprise Management: The Complex Past of the Evolving Present," Contemporary China, Vol. III, No. III, p. 85.

71. David Bonavia, "In Economy, Learn from Sichuan," Far Eastern Economic Review, 21 November 1980, p. 31.

72. RMRB, 24 July 1980, p. 2.

73. Ch'en Yung-sheng, "Zhao Ziyang and His Sichuan Experience," Issues and Studies (Taipei, October 1980), p. 31.

74. Hoshino Kyoji, "China's New Economic Policy as Viewed From Sichuan," Ta Kung Pao (Hong Kong), 16 July 1980, p. 3.

75. Liu Hsiang-chi, "An Integrated Enterprise of Agriculture, Industry, and Commerce: A New-Born Thing in China," Economic Reporter (Hong Kong), No. 1667, 30 April 1980, p. 25.

76. Shu Shin-wang, "The Rise of Zhao Ziyang," China Report (New Delhi, November/December 1980), p. 4.

77. Ch'en Yung-sheng, "Zhao Ziyang and His Sichuan Experience."

78. See for example the interview with Xue Muqiao, director of the State Planning Commission's Economic Research Institute, China Business Review, Vol. VIII, No. IV (July-August 1981), pp. 58-60.

79. See the "Communique of the Third Plenum" in Beijing Review, No. 52, 29 December 1978, pp. 6-16; and "The Political Significance of the Third Plenum," Issues and Studies (February 1979), pp. 1-10.

80. "Communique," ibid., p. 12.

81. For the partially translated text of Zhao's work report titled "Strive to Speed Up Socialist Modernization in Sichuan," see FBIS (15 and 22 February 1979), pp. J1-14; the full text is carried in SCRB, 15 February

1979, and is translated in Shambaugh (Ed.), "Zhao Ziyang's 'Sichuan Experience,' " pp. 93-126.

82. Ibid.

83. Ibid.

84. For the full text see SCRB, 31 January 1979; partial translation in FBIS (1 February 1979), pp. J2-3.

85. For the full text see SCRB, 5 February 1979; partial translation in FBIS (6 February 1979), pp. J1-2.

86. Beijing XHDS, 9 March 1979, FBIS (12 March 1979), pp. J2-3.

87. CSPS, 8 March 1979, FBIS (15 March 1979), p. J1.

88. CSPS, 12 March 1979, FBIS (15 March 1979), p. J1.

89. CSPS, 6 February 1979, FBIS (9 February 1979), pp. J4-5.

90. CSPS, 18 February 1979, FBIS (23 February 1979), p. J5.

91. CSPS, 3 March 1979, FBIS (5 March 1979), p. J1.

92. CSPS, 18 March 1979, FBIS (20 March 1979), p. Q1.

93. CSPS, 12 March 1979, FBIS (23 March 1979), p. L15.

94. Tao Siliang, "A Letter Sent Out at Last—To My Father, Tao Zhu," Renmin Ribao (hereafter RMRB), 10 December 1978, FBIS (14 December 1978), pp. E2-5.

95. Ibid.

96. RMRB, 23 March 1979, FBIS (2 April 1979), pp. L11-18; and SCRB, 24 March 1979.

97. CSPS, 22 February 1979, FBIS (2 March 1979), pp. J2-3.

98. Ibid., pp. J3-5.

99. For an analysis of this period see Chinese Political Debate Since the Third Plenum, FBIS Analysis Report, No. FB 79-10017 (1 August 1979).

100. See for example "Commentator" articles in the 13 April Wen Hui Bao; 22 April Jiefang Ribao; 21 April Nanfang Ribao; and 26 April Jiangxi Ribao.

101. Zheng Ming (Hong Kong), No. 31, 1 May 1980. It should be noted that a survey of the major national newspapers and journals reveals no such article, and Zheng Ming does not cite its source.

102. See for example RMRB, 25 February 1979, FBIS (8 March 1979), pp. J1-3; Beijing XHDS, 16 March, FBIS (19 March 1979), pp. L15-17.

103. See for example "To Realize the Four Modernizations We Must Bring Into Full Play the Role of Existing Enterprises," SCRB (4 June 1979); "Carry Out the Struggle Against the Ultra-Leftist Line and Properly Implement Agricultural Policy," SCRB (9 June 1979); "We Must Raise the Quality of Products," SCRB (10 June 1979); "Increase Savings to Increase Production," SCRB (13 June 1979); "We Must Promote Light Industry and Textile Production," SCRB (14 June 1979); "Adjusting the National Economy Is the Key in Turning Passivity into Activism," SCRB (15 June 1979); "Make

Painstaking Efforts to Bring New Land Under Cultivation," SCRB (17 June 1979); and "Properly Carry Out Agricultural Production Policy," SCRB (25 June 1979).

104. Beijing XHDS, 17 April 1979, FBIS (19 April 1979), p. Q1.

105. CSPS, 29 March 1979, FBIS (5 April 1979), p. Q1.

106. Beijing XHDS, 17 April 1979, FBIS (19 April 1979), p. Q1.

107. Beijing XHDS, 22 May 1979, FBIS (23 May 1979), pp. Q1-5.

108. See "Strengthen the Party Discipline and Inspection," SCRB, 3 June 1979.

109. Beijing XHDS, 16 and 17 June 1979, FBIS (19 June 1979), p. G3.

110. Beijing XHDS, 1 July 1979, FBIS (3 July 1979), pp. G4-5. This trip was also well-covered in SCRB, notably the 17 and 21 July issues.

111. CSPS, 31 July 1979, FBIS (1 August 1979), p. Q1.

112. For the Communique of the Fourth Plenum see Beijing Review, No. 40, 5 October 1979, pp. 32-34.

113. Qian Taigang, "Zhao Ziyang's Critical Biography."

114. Beijing XHDS, 5 October 1979, FBIS (5 October 1979), pp. L12-13. For full text see FBIS Supplement (25 October 1979).

115. Zhao's lack of attendance at these important meetings is revealed in: (provincial conference), CSPS, 21 October 1979 and FBIS (23 October 1979), p. Q1; and (central-level congress), Beijing XHDS, 19 October 1979 and FBIS (22 October 1979), p. L6.

116. CSPS, 25 December 1979, FBIS (7 January 1980), pp. Q1-3.

117. Zhongguo Baike Nian Jian (Shanghai, 1980), p. 109.

118. Reprinted in 6 January 1980 SCRB. For full translated text see CSPS, 5 January 1980, FBIS (9 January 1980), pp. Q1-3.

119. Ibid., pp. Q1-2.

120. Ibid., p. Q3.

121. Guangming Ribao (hereafter GMRB), 12 January 1980, p. 1. Translation carried in JPRS Report: Sociological, Education, Culture (January 1980), pp. 104-5.

122. Ibid.

123. See "New Acting Head of Chinese Government," New York Times, 25 April 1980, p. A8.

124. GMRB via Beijing XHDS, 10 August 1979, FBIS (10 August 1979), p. Q1.

125. See, respectively: Beijing XHDS, 14 August 1979 and FBIS (15 August 1979), p. Q1; and GMRB, 15 July 1979, p. 1. For translation see FBIS (23 July 1979), p. Q1.

126. These statistics are calculated from a number of sources by Kenneth Walker in his "China's Grain Production 1952-57 and 1975-80: Some Basic Statistics," China Quarterly, No. 86 (June 1981), pp. 226, 229.

127. Beijing XHDS, 5 September 1980, FBIS (9 September 1980), pp. L12-13.

7
Zhao Ziyang's Career and Elite Mobility in the Chinese Political System

What does Zhao Ziyang's career development tell us about paths to the top of the Chinese political hierarchy? More specifically, what does it tell us about channels of recruitment, credentials for advancement, political socialization, and transformation of elites in the Chinese political system? To be sure, a single case study is hardly optimal to posit any firm conclusions about these large questions. Nevertheless, Zhao's career is illustrative and it largely concurs with other case studies of Chinese elites.[1] However, every case has it own unique features. There exists no guaranteed formula to propel one up the career ladder. Different strategies for advancement have proven effective at different points in time. Zhao's career has spanned a period characterized by recurrent political upheaval, and he has had to adjust his strategies accordingly in order to survive. What follows is an attempt to summarize the various factors which affected (or did not affect) Zhao's career development, and to place his career in the broader context of Chinese elite mobility.

Essentially there exist formal and informal channels of recruitment and advancement in the Chinese political hierarchy. Formal channels are institutional, while informal channels include one's affiliations and credentials.

Zhao Ziyang advanced to the summit of the political system through the one formal channel most likely to get him there—the Party. Moreover, Zhao was brought into the Party through another formal channel, the Communist Youth League (CYL). The CYL is not the only source of recruitment into the Party (e.g., trade unions, mass organizations, campaigns), but it is the most common and important one. As we have seen in this study, the vast majority of Zhao's jobs during his career were in the CCP bureaucratic system (xitong). Whether he was working in the Rural Work Department, Secretariat, "Four Clean-ups" Office, etc., the Party was Zhao's boss. This is significant because his allegiances were not split between the Party and another functional bureaucratic system, i.e, another ministry. Unlike many CCP cadres, Zhao did not maintain dual portfolios in more than one <u>xitong</u>. It should be quickly noted that the two exceptions to this rule in Zhao's career were his stints as chief of the Guangdong Grain Procurement Bureau (subordinate to the Ministry of Grain) and as PLA political commissar in the Guangzhou and Chengdu Military Regions (subordinate to the PLA General Political Department). However, neither of these positions lasted long enough for Zhao to build an independent power base. This was a mixed blessing. While he did not threaten his CCP constituents with a rival source of power, neither did another organization provide him sanctuary or support during troubled times. When the Party, or elements within it, were not able to support Zhao, he had no real alternative. Thus we may conclude that Zhao's institutional power was based in the CCP rather than in a state bureaucracy.[2] This was probably an influential factor in the selection of Zhao for Premier, i.e, in managing the State Council he would have no ministerial conflict of interest.

In addition to political parties and the bureaucracy, it has been suggested that local government is a third institutional channel of elite recruitment.[3] While the majority of China's post-revolution, first-generation leadership went straight from the battlefield to Zhongnanhai,[4] a striking characteristic about the leadership now emerging is that much of their careers have been spent in local, provincial, or regional government.[5] This development, it is worth noting, is consistent with second- and third-generation elites in the Soviet Union, many of whom have spent time as <u>obkom</u> (regional) Party secretaries.

By having worked in the provinces Zhao Ziyang not only learned local realities first-hand and built up administrative expertise, but he also gained seniority. In China seniority is rewarded. So-called "helicopter promotions" inevitably fall. Moreover, by working in the provinces, Zhao was able to cultivate a regional base of power. He was able to do so in two ways: with respect to the center, and with respect to the populace. He was able to gain support from above and below. Zhao was able to advance his career by capitalizing on the center's needs in Guangdong and Sichuan. Both provinces possess a large-scale and diversified economy, and are located far enough from the center to make operational control difficult. As a result, Zhao was placed in the pivotal positions of arbiter and bargainer between central and local interests. The difficult task of reconciling their respective interests involves both satisfying local needs and assuring central authorities that their orders are being carried out. For example, while convincing the center that "localism" was being kept under control, Zhao in fact promoted local interests by implementing economic policies which fostered decentralization and regional prosperity. In fact, both Guangdong and Sichuan provinces became "cellular" economic units quite capable of maintaining growth without large central investment.[6]

Increased production is clearly in local interests, a policy that Zhao Ziyang has consistently stood for throughout his career.

Herein lies the foundation of Zhao's regional base of support. While it is impossible to measure precisely, I believe that Zhao enjoys broad popular support among the "masses." This is due to the economic policies (especially the "responsibility system" in agriculture) which he has implemented and become identified with. As was noted in Chapter 6, the Sichuan peasants were fond of saying, "If you want to eat, see Zhao Ziyang" (Ni yao chiliang, kan Zhao Ziyang). One may well ask whether popular support matters in an authoritarian system of one-party rule? I suggest that it does. Even in a one-party system the regime needs to maintain its legitimacy, and the best way to do so is to increase the standard of living of the populace. Zhao's policies have done this and it has earned him widespread support among the peasantry—which in China is a constituency not to be overlooked. The CCP came to power because of peasant support; if it is to stay in power it needs to maintain that support. This bodes well for Zhao's chances of staying in power after Deng Xiaoping leaves the scene, even though Zhao's bureaucratic and clientalistic bases of power seem less strong.

Having examined Zhao's formal channels of recruitment, let us now examine the informal channels and credentials which Zhao used to rise through the system. Throughout this study we have noted the importance of guanxi and clientalism. Patron-client networks are present in all political systems, but perhaps nowhere are they more important than in China. These ties can be based on a number of factors, but common socializing experiences are the most durable. The "old boy network" in the Chinese Communist Party is not based on having attended the "right" schools or being the child of a member of the elite. Rather, the CCP elite were schooled on the battlefield during the anti-Japanese and civil wars, and during the numerous campaigns of the Maoist era (most notably the Cultural Revolution). These socializing experiences provided a lasting bond for those who survived. To have been on the Long March and/or fought against the Japanese provided an almost automatic entree to the CCP elite. As we saw in Chapter 1, Zhao fought against the Japanese and served under several individuals who became national elites after 1949.

After the revolution Zhao continued to serve under key leaders in the Central-South Bureau and, of course, Tao Zhu, in the Guangdong CCP apparatus. Zhao's ties to Tao Zhu represent two types of patron-client networks in the Chinese system. The first is a direct one-to-one relationship whereby the patron promotes and protects the client. Zhao's promotions up through the Guangdong Party apparatus to become first secretary can be directly attributed to Tao Zhu's support. Similarly, Tao offered Zhao protection during the early stages of the Cultural Revolution when he kept Zhao abreast of the unfolding events at the center and counseled him on tactics for survival. Having this kind of patron can, however, be a double-edged sword, i.e., a secure central patron can protect and promote a provincial client, but conversely a vulnerable central patron can destabilize a client and they may fall from power together. This was the fate of Tao Zhu and Zhao Ziyang in January 1967. Deng Xiaoping has also been Zhao's direct patron, but I would argue only during the post-Cultural Revolution period. While they had contact in the 1950s (and this is when Zhao probably first came to Deng's attention), the evidence does not suggest a close relationship at that time. The second type of patron-client network is less direct and more ambiguous, but more common. This is a network of interlocking ties whereby a client can reap the benefits of his patron's relationships with higher officials. In Zhao's case, he was able to benefit (at varying times) from Tao Zhu's ties to Mao Zedong, Lin Biao, and Liu Shaoqi.

Despite the central importance of <u>guanxi</u> as a channel of recruitment in the Chinese system, patron-client ties alone cannot insure job security in a political system as fluid as the Chinese system has been since 1949. As the cases of Hua Guofeng, Ji Dengkui, and the "Gang of Four" illustrate, one must have more to sustain himself after their patron leaves the scene. This point should not be lost on Zhao Ziyang, who needs to diversify his power base to improve his chances of surviving after Deng Xiaoping departs. Zhao currently does not have a strong network of provincial clients directly beholden to him, and inheriting Deng's clients is problematic.

It is a striking fact in Zhao's career that while he has had patrons, he has not had many clients. During his tenure in Guangdong only Li Ziyuan can be considered a true client, insofar as his own career paralleled Zhao's very closely and he was the only official from Guangdong to go to Sichuan with Zhao. Zhao's other colleagues in Guangdong maintained their own stature and had independent ties to Tao Zhu and other leaders, e.g., Ou Mengjue, Lin Liming, Wang Kuang, Wang Lanxi, and Liu Tianfu. During Zhao's tenure in Sichuan only Du Xingyuan can be considered Zhao's client, and even then his allegiances may be tied equally to Deng. Du served as a deputy Party secretary under Zhao in Sichuan and was named secretary-general of the State Council at the same time that Zhao was named Premier. He was dismissed from this post in June 1983. Two other possible clients from Sichuan are Zhao Cangbi (dismissed as Minister of Public Security in June 1983) and Duan Junyi (current first Party Secretary of Beijing Municipality). However, Zhao Cangbi was transferred out of Sichuan two years prior to Zhao Ziyang's own transfer to Beijing and Duan Junyi left in December 1976 (before his current post he served as Minister of Railways from February 1977 to November 1978 when he was named first Party secretary in Henan, a position in which he served until January 1981). An Pingsheng, the current first secretary of Yunnan province, may also be considered a client of Zhao's. They worked closely together on agricultural matters in Guangdong during the 1950s before An was transferred to neighboring Guangxi in 1961. Finally there is Yang Rudai, the current "leading" secretary of Sichuan, who was promoted from subprovincial obscurity to the leading organs of the province in 1977 while Zhao was first secretary. While Zhao had to acquiesce to such an appointment, it is unclear what exact role he played in Yang's promotion.

To this point we have determined that both formal institutional and informal clientalistic channels permitted Zhao Ziyang to rise to the top of the Chinese political hierarchy. These channels are _systemic_ factors affecting career development. What are the _idiosyncratic_ factors involved? In addition to the importance of common socializing experiences and seniority already discussed, three factors are important: professional competance, visibility, and opportunism.

Professional competance (skills and on-the-job performance) does make a difference in advancing—or stalling—a career in the Chinese political system. Upward mobility is not just the result of the factors outlined above; there is no conveyor belt one can ride to the top if one has the right patron and power base. Merit is therefore a key variable in one's career.

One must be, at the same time, a policy generalist and specialist. These are not mutually exclusive. Being a policy generalist does not mean being a dilettante; it means being a specialist in several policy issue areas with special expertise in one or two. It pays to have worked in several issue areas. Those who only work in one or a few issue areas do not rise to the top as a rule, although they may rise to mid-level bureaucratic positions in their functional area of expertise. Societies are complex; issues are multiple and overlapping; vested interests and demands know no limit, while resources are finite. Therefore, a leader must be able to comprehend the complexity and interrelationships between issues, while satisfying many diverse groups and sectors of society and government. If the leader's background has not prepared him to intelligently comprehend a variety of issue areas, he is severely handicapped in his job—and probably would not have a leadership position in the first place. Moreover, as economic modernization becomes the major national goal, technical expertise increases as a requirement for admission to the political elite. The "technocrat" emerges.

As his provincial career progressed, Zhao Ziyang continually expanded the range of issue areas in which he worked. By the time he was named Premier in 1980 he had worked on science policy, education, industrial management, foreign policy, Party rectification and recruitment, information management, birth control, trade unions, sports, ideology and propaganda, personnel management, political-military relations, water conservancy and forestry, women's issues, youth, and of course a host of issues associated with agriculture.

Agriculture has undoubtedly been Zhao's specialty throughout his career. He is truly an agricultural expert; he understands both technical and managerial facets. While being knowledgeable about agriculture is not a mandatory criterion for upward elite mobility in China, it is certainly useful. Agriculture has always been, and continues to be, the most important sector of the Chinese economy. As such, it has always been of primary concern to Chinese leaders and a primary locus of political conflict among them. Without a working knowledge of agriculture, a leader cannot understand the core realities of eighty percent of the populace. Further, inadequate food supply is a major threat to domestic stability. Despite China's impressive capacity to meet its basic food needs, there is never an adequate surplus. Thus there is constant potential for social upheaval which would threaten not only the tenuous social fabric, but also the regime's legitimacy.

The second idiosyncratic factor affecting career development is visibility. One must be active at conferences, in campaigns, and in the media if higher elites are to take note. The more attention one receives in the central media, the better the chances of promotion to the center. However, "overexposure" in the provincial media can be interpreted by the center as building an "independent kingdom." It is useful though if one appears to be dealing with issues of importance to the center. It also helps to work in a model unit, strategic locale, or growth sector of the economy, because one can reap political capital from economic success. If one produces results, others will gravitate toward him and will help to secure his power base.

Zhao Ziyang's career confirms these points. He frequently appeared at and addressed meetings, was an activist for many campaigns, published articles, was frequently reported in the provincial and central press, took publicized "inspection tours," met foreign visitors and traveled abroad. He was a pacesetter in implementing economic reforms when the center wanted to use Sichuan as a testing place for new policies, and his career certainly benefitted from the success of the "Sichuan experiment."

The third idiosyncratic factor is opportunism. The extreme oscillating nature of the Chinese political system over the past thirty years has fostered and necessitated opportunism as a survival tactic for cadres. It is a basic rule of the political game. Chinese cadres must be able to ascertain shifts in policy, monitor the fate of key leaders, and respond accordingly. If one can anticipate a policy change or purge, one can position oneself to benefit by it (or at least not be hurt by it), or can simply lie low until the atmosphere grows more favorable. To be sure, this has also produced extreme cautiousness and lethargy in the Chinese polity. Most cadres have learned that it pays to do as little as possible. Taking initiative can be dangerous. This constitutes, in my opinion, one of the major impediments to China's quest for modernity. The present regime first tried to cope with this problem by purging those opportunists they identified as the "wind faction" (fengpai), i.e., those who rode the political wind in whichever direction it blew. Next, the Deng regime promised no more campaigns and recently began the long-awaited "rectification" (purge) of Party members who are inefficient or had been overzealous during the Cultural Revolution. Over half of the 40 million member strong CCP joined during the Cultural Revolution decade and stand to have their credentials reexamined. During Mao's lifetime one had, in fact, to act opportunistically (or one could say with "flexibility") to survive politically.

Zhao Ziyang, as we have witnessed throughout this study, was no different. His mere survival in the Chinese political system since 1949 is testimony to the fact that he learned this rule very well. Zhao has clearly been an opportunist during his provincial career. We have seen this repeatedly in his speeches, articles, and frequent "disappearances" from public view during periods of leftist policy. Having said this, however, we must also conclude that he said and did no more than he had to in order to survive—with the possible exception of his behavior during the Socialist Education Movement. His preferred tactic during leftist periods was to maintain a low profile and/or to mouth the necessary rhetoric while promoting production in practice.

Finally, we turn to the question of what Zhao Ziyang's rise to the premiership means in terms of elite transformation. Does his appointment represent a broader phenomemon? Is the composition of the Chinese elite changing, and have the credentials for promotion to the top elite changed?

First of all, Zhao's appointment as Premier represents a slight generational change among the Chinese elite. Sixty-one years of age at the time of his appointment, Zhao was about fifteen years junior to most other high-ranking leaders at that time. We might distinguish between a "Long March" generation and a "kang zhan" generation (War of Resistance Against Japan). Zhao belongs to the latter. Zhao's age concurs with those newly elected to the Twelfth Central Committee,[7] and affirms the CCP's avowed policy to promote "younger" leaders.

Second, Zhao's appointment indicates a shift from ideologues to managerial bureaucrats—the apparatchik. This phenomenom may be new to Chinese elites, but it simply confirms the trend evident for some time in Eastern Europe and the Soviet Union.[8] The catalyst for this process is economic development. As a country modernizes, bureaucracy inexorably proliferates in response to the administrative needs of the state and society. The needed type of managerial bureaucrat is not only a skilled administrator capable of managing policies and people, but is also versed in technical aspects of the economy. This "technocrat" has most likely acquired his skills through long service in the hinterland while serving in the provincial Party apparatus.[9] As a result of this long service in the interior of the country, the technocrat is quite parochial in his outlook. He is much more likely to be concerned with sub-national issues and constituencies than national or international ones.

Zhao Ziyang personifies this elite type. He is well versed in several facets of China's economy, but is primarily an agriculture specialist. He has worked for his entire career in the provinces and his major constituency is the Chinese peasantry. He has proven himself an efficient administrator in the Party apparatus. He diverges somewhat from the "parochial" stereotype, however, because throughout his career he met with foreigners, although he never traveled abroad until 1978. Foreigners who have met Zhao invariably comment on his urbane and sometimes jovial manner, his quick mind and articulateness.[10] Nevertheless, before becoming Premier he never spoke or wrote publicly about international affairs, and has never articulated his vision of China as a modern society. His commentaries on China's quest for modernity have been limited to particular aspects of economic development.

By the standards of socialist countries, however, Zhao Ziyang must be considered a very liberal economic thinker. He favors decentralization of decision-making, the use of material incentives, private enterprise, a promotion system based on merit, enterprise accountability pegged to profits and losses, and many more policies which were anathema to his predecessors. Above all, Zhao stands for increasing output and bettering the well-being of the populace. Like Deng Xiaoping, he wants results. Just as Deng did not care whether a cat was black or white, as long as it caught mice, Zhao Ziyang also has a quotation which captures his economic philosophy: "Socialism means two things: public ownership of the means of production and paying each according to his work. As long as these two principles are safeguarded we should feel free to adopt all those structures, systems, policies, and measures which can promote the development of production, and not bind ourselves as silkworms do within cocoons."[11]

NOTES

1. Gorden A. Bennett, "Elite and Society in China: A Summary of Research and Interpretation," in Robert Scalapino (Ed.), Elites in the People's Republic of China (Seattle, 1972), pp. 3-37; Parris Chang, "Provincial Party Leaders' Strategies for Survival During the Cultural Revolution," in Scalapino, Elites in the People's Republic of China, pp. 501-39; Lowell Dittmer, "Bases of Power in Chinese Politics: A Theory and Analysis of the Fall of the 'Gang of Four,' " World Politics (October 1978), pp. 26-60; Nina

Halpern, "Elites in the People's Republic of China: A Survey of the Literature," unpublished manuscript; David M. Lampton, "Comrade: Paths to Power in China," unpublished manuscript; Andrew J. Nathan, "A Factionalism Model for CCP Politics," China Quarterly, No. 51 (July-September 1972), pp. 444-74; Michel Oksenberg, "Paths to Leadership in Communist China," Current Scene, 1 August 1965, pp. 1-11; Michel Oksenberg, "Local Leaders in Rural China, 1962-65: Individual Attributes, Bureaucratic Positions, and Political Recruitment," in A. Doak Barnett (Ed.), Chinese Communist Politics in Action (Seattle, 1969), pp. 155-215; Michel Oksenberg, "The Exit Pattern From Chinese Politics and Its Implications," China Quarterly, No. 67 (September 1976), pp. 501-18; Michel Oksenberg and Yeung Sai-cheung, "Hua Guofeng's Pre-Cultural Revolution Hunan Years, 1949-66: The Making of a Political Generalist," China Quarterly, No. 69 (March 1977), pp. 3-53; William L. Parish Jr., "Factions in Chinese Military Politics," China Quarterly, No. 56 (October 1973), pp. 667-99; Robert Putnam, The Comparative Study of Political Elites (Englewood Cliffs, 1976); Thomas Robinson, "Lin Biao as an Elite Type," in Scalapino (Ed.), Elites in the People's Republic of China, pp. 149-75; Frederick Teiwes, Provincial Party Personnel in Mainland China, 1956-66; Tsou Tang, "Prolegomenon to the Study of Informal Groups in CCP Politics," China Quarterly, No. 65 (March 1976), pp. 98-111; William Whitson and Chen-hsia Huang, The Chinese High Command (New York, 1973).

2. There are those who would argue that the Communist Party is the state in a socialist system. My distinction is based on the concept of functional bureaucratic systems (discussed in the Introduction) as a source of competing interest groups. I do not accept the idea that socialist countries are monolithic, totalitarian states with all power vested in the Party elite. Rather I believe that rival interest groups, based on functional professions, compete for power. This concept is best articulated in Gordon H. Skilling and Franklyn Griffiths, Interest Groups and Soviet Politics (Princeton, 1971).

3. Robert Putnam, The Comparative Study of Political Elites, pp. 49-51.

4. The location of the main offices of the Chinese leadership in Beijing.

5. See Hong Yung Lee, "China's 12th Central Committee: Rehabilitated Cadres and Technocrats," Asian Survey (June 1983).

6. For an elaboration of this concept see Audrey Donnithorne, China's Economic System (London, 1967).

7. Ibid., p. 684.

8. See John Kautsky, Communism and the Politics of Development: Persistent Myths and Changing Behavior (New York, 1968); Gordon H. Skilling and Franklyn Griffiths, Interest Groups in Soviet Politics

(Princeton, 1971); Jerry Hough, The Soviet Prefects: The Local Party Organs in Industrial Decision-Making (Cambridge, 1969); Harold D. Lasswell and Daniel Lerner, World Revolutionary Elites (Cambridge, 1965); Richard Lowenthal, "Development vs. Utopia in Communist Policy," in Chalmers Johnson, Change in Communist Systems (Stanford, 1970); Richard Lowenthal, "The Ruling Party in a Mature Society," in Marx Field (Ed.), Social Consequences of Modernization in Communist Societies (Baltimore, 1976).

9. For a discussion of this phenomenon see Robert Putnam, The Comparative Study of Political Elites, pp. 210-11.

10. We know very little about Zhao's personal qualities and private life. We do know that he was married to Liang Baiqi, who was a former low-level CCP cadre in Guangdong before the Cultural Revolution. It is not known if Liang has been his only wife or if she is still alive, since she has not been seen in public since before the Cultural Revolution. They are believed to have five sons and one daughter. Two of the sons were reportedly accused of profiteering and abusing their father's influence in 1981. Zhao was said to have reprimanded them and made a self-criticism in front of the Politburo. Red Guard sources claimed that Zhao's hobbies included raising tropical fish, watching films, and dancing to Western music. He has further revealed to visitors in recent years that he jogs regularly and enjoys playing bridge. Zhao does not speak any foreign languages.

11. "The Sichuan Experiment With Enterprises," Beijing Review, No. 14 (6 April 1981), p. 21.

Bibliography

Chinese Primary Sources

Da Gongbao, Hong Kong
Dang Dai, Hong Kong
Gongshang Ribao, Hong Kong
Guangming Ribao, Beijing
Guangzhou Keji Zhanbao, Guangzhou
Guangzhou Hongweibing, Guangzhou
Hongqi, Beijing
Hongqibao, Guangzhou
Hongqi Ruhua, Guangzhou
Hongse Zao Fanzhe, Guangzhou
Ji Da Gelian, Guangzhou
Jiangxi Ribao, Nanchang
Jiefang Ribao, Shanghai
Kuangbiao, Guangzhou
Lishi Yanjiu, Beijing
Mao Zedong Sixiang Wansui!
Minzu Tuanjie, Beijing
Nanfang Ribao, Guangzhou
Nianqing Zhanshi, Guangzhou
Renmin Ribao, Beijing
San Zhaobao, Guangzhou
Shangyu, Guangzhou
Shengzhi Hongqi, Guangzhou
Shoudu Hongweibing, Beijing
Shi Shi Shouce, Beijing
Sichuan Ribao, Chengdu
Wen Huibao, Hong Kong
Wen Huibao, Shanghai

Xiao Bing, Guangzhou
Xinwen Zhance, Guangzhou
Xinhuashe, Beijing, Guangzhou
Yangcheng Wanbao, Guangzhou
Yi Yue Fengbao, Guangzhou
Ye Zhanbao, Guangzhou
Zhandou Wenyi, Guangzhou
Zheng Ming, Hong Kong
Zhongda Zhanbao, Guangzhou
Zhongda Hongqi, Guangzhou
Zhonggong Minglu, Taibei
Zhongguo Baike Nianjian, Shanghai
Zhongguo Qingnianbao, Beijing

English Primary Sources

Appearances and Activities of Leading Chinese Personalities
Beijing Review
China Aktuell Supplement, PRC Official Activities
China News Analysis
Chinese Law and Government
Chinese Science and Technology
Communist China Digest
Current Background
Current Scene
Foreign Broadcast Information Service Special Report on Communist Media
Foreign Broadcast Information Service Daily Report—Eastern Europe
Foreign Broadcast Information Service Daily Report—China
Joint Publications Research Service Report
News from Chinese Regional Radio Stations
Survey of Mainland China Magazines
Survey of Mainland China Press
Union Research Service, Who's Who in Communist China
U.S. Consulate General (Hong Kong) Biographic Card File

Japanese Primary Sources

Japanese Foreign Ministry, Xiandai Zhongguo Renmin Zidian (Tokyo: Foreign Ministry, Asia Division, 1972).

English Secondary Sources

Ahn, Byung-joon. Chinese Politics and the Cultural Revolution. Seattle: University of Washington Press, 1976.

Barnett, A. Doak. Cadres, Bureaucracy and Political Power in Communist China. New York: Columbia University Press, 1967.

————. Communist China: The Early Years, 1949-1955. New York: Praeger Publishers, 1964.

Baum, Richard. Prelude to Revolution: Mao, the Party, and the Peasant Question, 1962-66. New York: Columbia University Press, 1975.

Baum, Richard and Frederick Teiwes. Ssu-Ch'ing: The Socialist Education Movement of 1962-66. Berkeley: University of California Press, 1968.

Bennett, Gordon. "Elites and Society in China: A Summary of Research and Interpretation." Robert Scalapino (Ed.), Elites in the People's Republic of China. Seattle: University of Washington Press, 1972.

Bennett, Gordon and Ronald Monteperto. Red Guard: The Political Biography of Dai Hsiao-ai. New York: Doubleday and Co., 1971.

Bernstein, Thomas. Leadership and Mobilization in the Collectivization of Agriculture in China and Russia: A Comparison. Ph.D. dissertation, Columbia University, 1970.

Bonavia, David. "In Economy, Learn from Sichuan." Far Eastern Economic Review, 21 November 1981.

Chamberlain, Heath B. "Transition and Consolidation in Urban China: A Study of Leaders and Organizations in Three Cities, 1949-53." Robert Scalapino (Ed.), Elites in the People's Republic of China. Seattle: University of Washington Press, 1972.

Chang, Parris. Power and Policy in China. University Park: Pennsylvania State University Press, 2d ed., 1978.

————. "Provincial Party Leaders' Strategies for Survival During the Cultural Revolution." Robert Scalapino (Ed.), Elites in the People's Republic of China. Seattle: University of Washington Press, 1972.

————. "Research Notes on the Changing Loci of Decision-Making in the CCP." China Quarterly, No. 44 (1970).

Charles, David. "The Dismissal of Marshal Peng Dehuai." China Quarterly, No. 8 (October-December 1961).

Ch'en Yung-sheng. "Zhao Ziyang and His Sichuan Experience." Issues and Studies (October 1980).

Dick, Glenn. "The General Political Department." William Whitson (Ed.), The Military and Political Power in China in the 1970s. New York: Praeger Publishers, 1972.

Dittmer, Lowell. "Bases of Power in Chinese Politics: A Theory and Analysis of the Fall of the 'Gang of Four.' " World Politics (October 1978).

————. Liu Shao-ch'i and the Cultural Revolution: The Politics of Mass Criticism. Berkeley: University of California Press, 1974.

Domes, Jurgen. China After the Cultural Revolution. Berkeley: University of California Press, 1977.

Donnithorne, Audrey. China's Economic System. London: Allen and Unwin, 1967.

Fox, Galen. Campaigning for Power in China: 1967-76. Ph.D. dissertation, Princeton University, 1979.

Goldman, Merle. China's Intellectuals: Advise and Dissent. Cambridge: Harvard University Press, 1981.

Goodman, David, S. G. "Sichuan." Unpublished manuscript.

Halpern, Nina. "Elites in the People's Republic of China: A Survey of the Literature." Unpublished paper.

————. "Learning from Abroad: Chinese Views of the East European Economic Experience, 1977-1981." Unpublished paper.

Hersh, Seymour. The Price of Power: Kissinger in the Nixon White House. New York: Summit Books, 1983.

Hough, Jerry. The Soviet Prefects: The Local Party Origins in Industrial Decision-Making. Cambridge: Harvard University Press, 1969.

Kantsky, John. Communism and the Politics of Development: Persistent Myths and Changing Behavior. New York: John Wiley, 1968.

Kau, Ying-mao. "Patterns of Recruitment and Mobility of Urban Cadres." John Wilson Lewis (Ed.), The City in Communist China. Stanford: Stanford University Press, 1971.

Klein, Donald and Clark, Ann. Biographic Dictionary of Chinese Communism. Cambridge: Harvard University Press, 1971.

Lampton, David M. "Comrade: Paths to Power in China." Unpublished paper.

Lasswell, Harold and Daniel Lerner. World Revolutionary Elites. Cambridge: M.I.T. Press, 1965.

Lee, Hong Yung. "A Reply." China Quarterly, No. 70 (June 1977).

————. "China's 12th Central Committee: Rehabilitated Cadres and Technocrats." Asian Survey (June 1983).

————. The Politics of the Chinese Cultural Revolution. Berkeley: University of California Press, 1978.

Lieberthal, Kenneth. A Research Guide to Central Party and Government Meetings in China, 1949-1975. White Plains: M. E. Sharpe, 1976.

————. Central Documents and Politburo Politics. Ann Arbor: Michigan Papers in Chinese Studies, 1980.

————. "The Foreign Policy Debate in Peking as Seen Through Allegorical Articles, 1973-76." China Quarterly, No. 71 (September 1977).

Lowenthal, Richard. "Development vs. Utopia in Communist Policy." Chalmers Johnson (Ed.), Change in Communist Systems. Stanford: Stanford University Press, 1970.

--------. "The Ruling Party in a Mature Society." In Mark Field (Ed.), Social Consequences of Modernization in Communist Societies. Baltimore: Johns Hopkins University Press, 1976.

MacFarquhar, Roderick. The Hundred Flowers Campaign and the Chinese Intellectuals. New York: Praeger Publishers, 1960.

--------. The Origins of the Cultural Revolution, Vol. I. New York: Columbia University Press, 1974.

--------. The Origins of the Cultural Revolution, Vol. II: The Great Leap Forward. New York: Columbia University Press, 1983.

Mao Zedong. "On the Cooperative Transformation of Agriculture." Selected Works of Mao Zedong, Vol. V. Beijing: Foreign Languages Press, 1977.

Matthews, Thomas J. "The Cultural Revolution in Sichuan." Ezra Vogel (Ed.), The Cultural Revolution in the Provinces. Cambridge: Harvard University Press, 1971.

Moody, Peter R. "Policy and Power: The Career of Tao Zhu, 1956-1966." China Quarterly, No. 54 (1973).

Nathan, Andrew J. "A Factionalism Model for CCP Politics." China Quarterly, No. 51 (July-September 1972).

Oksenberg, Michel. "A Decade of Sino-American Relations." Foreign Affairs (Fall 1982).

--------. "Local Leaders in Rural China, 1962-1965." A. Doak Barnett (Ed.), Chinese Communist Politics in Action. Seattle: University of Washington Press, 1969.

--------. "Methods of Communication in the Chinese Bureaucracy." China Quarterly, No. 57 (January-March 1974).

--------. "Paths to Leadership in Communist China." Current Scene (August 1965).

--------. "The Chinese Policy Process and the Public Health Issue: An Arena Approach." Studies in Comparative Communism, Vol. VII, No. 4 (Winter 1974).

--------. "The Exit Pattern from Chinese Politics and Its Implications." China Quarterly, No. 67 (September 1976).

Oksenberg, Michel and Yeung Sai-cheung. "Hua Guofeng's Pre-Cultural Revolution Hunan Years, 1949-66: The Making of a Political Generalist." China Quarterly, No. 69 (January-March 1977).

Onate, Andre. "Hua Guofeng and the Arrest of the Gang of Four." China Quarterly, No. 75 (September 1978).

Parish, William L. "Factionalism in Chinese Military Politics." China Quarterly, No. 56 (October 1973).

Putnam, Robert. The Comparative Study of Political Elites. Englewood Cliffs: Prentice Hall, 1976.

Pye, Lucian. The Dynamics of Chinese Politics. Cambridge: Oelgeschlager, Gunn & Hain, Publishers, Inc., 1981.

Robinson, Thomas. "Lin Biao as an Elite Type." Robert Scalapino (Ed.), Elites in the People's Republic of China. Seattle: University of Washington Press, 1972.

Rosen, Stanley. Red Guard Factionalism and the Cultural Revolution in Guangzhou. Boulder: Westview Press, 1982.

--------. "The Democracy Movement in Guangzhou." Paper delivered to the Association for Asian Studies Annual Meeting, 1982.

--------. "The Radical Students in Guangdong During the Cultural Revolution." China Quarterly, No. 70 (June 1977).

Shambaugh, David. "The Role of the People's Liberation Army in Chinese Politics." Spring-Autumn Papers, Vol. III, No. 1. Ann Arbor: Centers for Chinese and Japanese Studies, 1981.

-------- (Ed.). "Zhao Ziyang's 'Sichuan Experience': Blueprint for a Nation." Chinese Law and Government, Vol. XV, No. 1 (Spring 1982).

Shu Shin-wang. "The Rise of Zhao Ziyang." China Report (November/ December 1980).

Shue, Vivienne. Peasant China in Transition. Berkeley: University of California Press, 1980.

Shurmann, Franz. Ideology and Organization in Communist China. Berkeley: University of California Press, 2d ed., 1966.

Skilling, Gordon H. and Franklyn Griffiths. Interest Groups and Soviet Politics. Princeton: Princeton University Press, 1971.

Teiwes, Frederick. Politics and Purges in China: Rectification and the Decline of Party Norms, 1950-1965. White Plains: M. E. Sharpe, 1979.

--------. Provincial Party Personnel in Mainland China, 1956-66. New York: Occassional Papers of the East Asian Institute at Columbia University, 1967.

Thurston, Anne. Authority and Legitimacy in Post-Revolution Rural Guangdong: The Case of the People's Communes. Ph.D. dissertation, University of California-Berkeley, 1975.

Tsou Tang. "Prolegomenon to the Study of Informal Groups in CCP Politics." China Quarterly, No. 65 (March 1976).

Union Research Institute. The Case of Peng Dehuai. Hong Kong: Union Research Service, 1968.

Vogel, Ezra. Canton Under Communism. Cambridge: Harvard University Press, 2d ed., 1980.

Walder, Andrew G. "Worker Participation in Enterprise Management: The Complex Past of the Evolving Present." Contemporary China, Vol. III, No. III.

Walker, Kenneth. "China's Grain Production 1952-57 and 1975-80: Some Basic Statistics." China Quarterly, No. 86 (June 1981).

Wayne, Earl A. "The Politics of Restaffing China's Provinces." Contemporary China (Spring 1978).

Whitson, William and Huang Chen-hsia. The Chinese High Command. New York: Praeger Publishers, 1973.

Yao, Mingle. The Conspiracy and Death of Lin Biao. New York: Alfred A. Knopf, 1983.

Zweig, David. "Context and Content in Policy Implementation: Household Contracts in China, 1977-1983." Unpublished paper.

————. "The Bei Da Debate on Education and the Fall of Deng Xiaoping." China Quarterly, No. 73 (March 1978).

Index

R0152005925

R0152005925   SSC   B
                        ZH65

        16.00

SHAMBAUGH, DAVID L
    MAKING OF A PREMIER
PAPER

R0152005925   SSC   B
                        ZH65

HOUSTON PUBLIC LIBRARY

CENTRAL LIBRARY
500 MCKINNEY